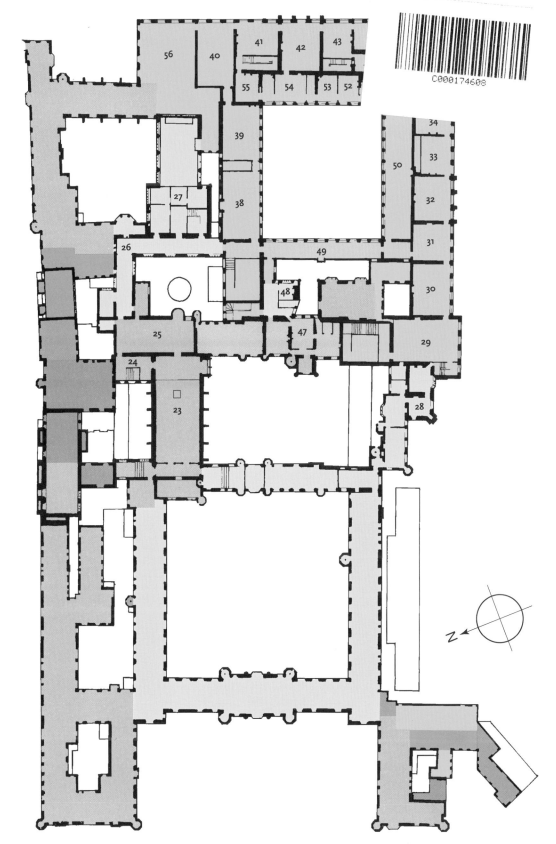

41

42 43

56 40

55 54 53 52

39

50 34

33

27 38 32

26 31

49

48 30

25 47

29

24

23 28

21

FIRST FLOOR

The Story of
Hampton Court Palace

The Story of Hampton Court Palace

David Souden
and
Lucy Worsley

MERRELL
LONDON · NEW YORK

In association with
Historic
Royal Palaces

Contents

Introduction

Before the days of helicopters, aeroplanes or even hot air balloons, Leonard Knyff was able to paint an astonishing bird's-eye view of the palace and gardens of Hampton Court in or around the year 1705 (fig. 2). In the centre of the picture stands the palace complex. It was, and remains, one of the country's most intriguing buildings. As the painting clearly shows, Hampton Court is really two palaces. The further half is the remaining portion of the magnificent red-brick palace, constructed for Cardinal Wolsey and Henry VIII in the early sixteenth century; the closer half is what was then the newly built Baroque palace containing the royal apartments, commissioned by William III and Mary II. Its 1300 rooms spread over 2.4 hectares (6 acres) in a complex of courtyards, cloisters and chambers.

The setting was as fine as the buildings, with 24 hectares (60 acres) of some of the most magnificent gardens: the avenues in Home Park in the foreground focusing on the elaborate Great Fountain Garden, the formal layout of the King's Privy Garden on the left and the intricate Wilderness on the right. Although some of the garden features have altered, and much of the surrounding area has been developed, this is still recognizably the view we see today. Many parts, including the world-famous Maze in the Wilderness, are precious survivals from a great age of gardening some three centuries ago.

Hampton Court Palace is one of the best-known buildings in Britain and one of the grandest. Its great West Front is one of the country's most recognizable edifices. The palace is ranked among the top British historic attractions, as it has been for almost two centuries. It is inextricably linked to Henry VIII, one of the most famous if also one of the most frightening of monarchs. Hampton Court was the setting for many nationally important events. Here Cardinal Wolsey entertained his king and foreign ambassadors. Henry VIII and most of his six wives held court in its grand interiors. Shakespeare and his players performed in the Great Hall, and the Authorized Version of the Bible was conceived here in 1604. Charles I escaped house arrest after his Civil War defeat. William and Mary brought French court etiquette and a new architectural style to the palace after 1689. In the eighteenth century, Georgian kings and princes argued violently amid its splendours. The court stopped using the palace after 1737 and it became instead a retirement home for courtiers and diplomats 'by the grace and favour' of the sovereign. They shared it with an increasing number of tourists. Since 1838, when Queen Victoria opened Hampton Court to the public, it has become a magnet for millions of visitors from Britain and abroad.

'Not in its stones nor in its gold is the greatest glory of a building, nor yet in its antiquity, but in the subtle spell that invests it by its association with those who in the past lived, thought and moved within its walls.' If you were to ask somebody interested in the past for the names of distinguished people associated with Hampton Court Palace, all the names above might be listed, but the name of Ernest Law, who wrote those words, would be less likely to come to mind. Yet through his efforts, at the end of the nineteenth century, the palace that we know today was essentially made, re-made and presented. These sentiments continue to animate the way the palace displays itself to the world. There were always quirky or unexpected characters alongside grand royal residents – whether Ernest Law himself, Sikh princesses who campaigned for women's suffrage, or George I's chocolate cook, not to mention the hundreds of people who have got lost in the Maze – and all have their part in the story.

Today Hampton Court Palace is a busy workplace. It is looked after by Historic Royal Palaces, the independent charity charged with conserving the 'unoccupied' royal palaces and helping people to learn more about all the stories described in these pages.

1. The West Front of Hampton Court Palace.

2. (overleaf) Detail of a bird's-eye view of Hampton Court Palace and gardens, c. 1705, by Leonard Knyff.

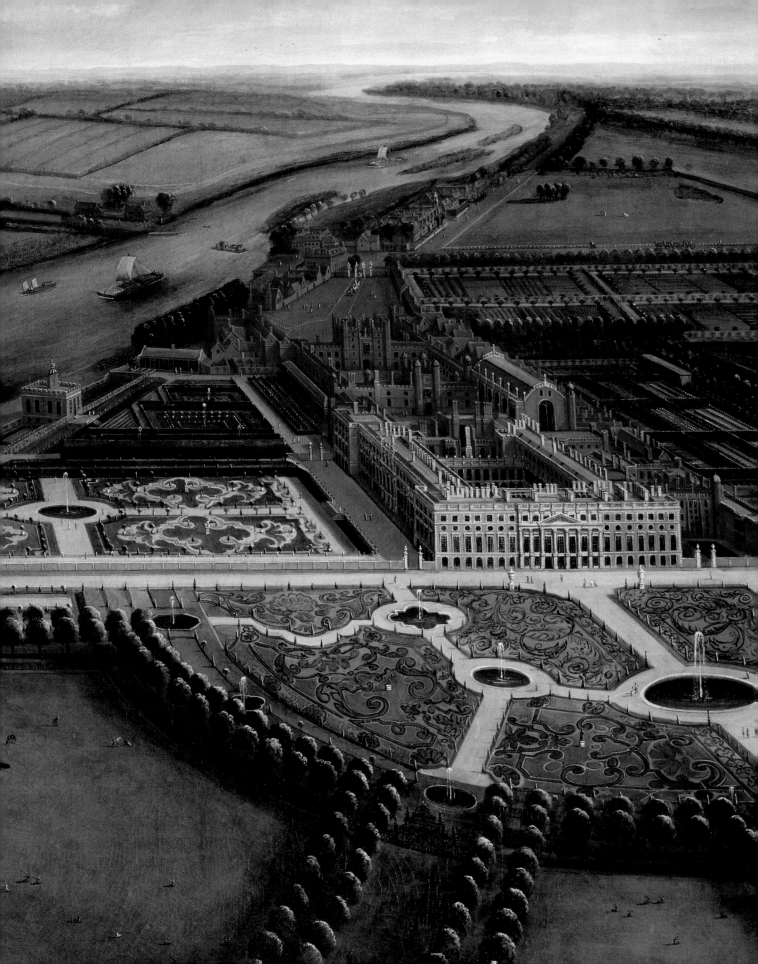

Life at Court

To understand Hampton Court Palace, it is essential to have some understanding of court life and the etiquette that underpinned it. The household of the king, the royal court, was for many centuries the political centre of the nation. At court, patronage and favour were given to those who pleased the monarch, and taken away from those who displeased him. All attention was centred on the monarch, who may actually have been seen by few but whose presence was tangible. This was expressed both in the architecture and the way in which the whole palace was physically arranged.

English kings had many houses, and the court moved with them (fig. 3). Before the days of regular parliaments and a modern constitutional monarchy, the national administration and treasury were functions of court and the royal household. Where the monarch resided, there was the court, and people of high social standing expected to participate as courtiers. These houses were physical expressions of both the ceremonial that was focused on royalty and the logistics for servicing a vast number of people. The biggest and best survivor from this period of royal life, Hampton Court was only one among many royal palaces in Tudor England. Henry VIII owned more than sixty houses, and the court would visit them for periods varying from a few hours to a few months.

3. (below) The arrival of Charles II and his bride, Catherine of Braganza, at Hampton Court in May 1662; a vivid illustration by Dirk Stoop of the scale of the royal court when on the move.

4. The King's Great Bedchamber was the grandest state room. In 1699 William III announced that in future all ambassadors were to be received at Hampton Court rather than at his London palaces, and he probably received ambassadors in the bedchamber, just as Charles II had done.

A place at court

The king on his throne sat at the centre of a vast and slowly revolving array of functionaries: personal attendants, councillors, visiting members of the aristocracy and their servants, sightseers and tradesmen. The long chains of rooms in the palace, one leading into another, acted like a filter. The guards at each successive doorway prevented the unworthy from penetrating into the king's inner rooms. Clothes played a vital part in the guards' decision whether

The Story of Hampton Court Palace

to let someone pass, and clothing consumed a high proportion of
a courtier's income.

Once inside the gates, the visitor found two main departments
of the court: the Lord Chamberlain's department, responsible for the
running of the state rooms, and the Lord Steward's department, the
'below stairs' areas of the palace such as the kitchens. When the king
was in residence, milling crowds pushed through the courtyards. There
could be as many as 800 people in attendance at Henry VIII's court. The
centre of life for most lower-ranking members of the court was the Great
Hall, where in Tudor times they dined in two shifts in the middle of the
day (fig. 5). Senior courtiers ate in the adjoining Great Watching Chamber
(fig. 6). Henry VIII himself ate in stately isolation in his dining room with
courtiers looking on; his dishes were produced in his own Privy Kitchen
rather than in the Great Kitchen serving the Great Hall (fig. 7).

Provisioning the royal household placed such a huge burden on the
surrounding countryside that the court could not remain for long. In
the later seventeenth century, the cost of feeding the whole of the royal

*5. (opposite) In this
perspective view of the
Great Hall engraved by
John Vardy in 1749 from a
drawing by William Kent,
the interior is shown as it
might have appeared in
the reign of Henry VIII
for the reception of
foreign ambassadors.*

*6. An imaginary view of
Cardinal Wolsey dining
with his household in the
Great Watching Chamber at
Hampton Court by Joseph
Nash, from* The Mansions
of England in the Olden
Time *(1839–49).*

household became prohibitive and the privilege was abolished for all but the grandest. Courtiers then had to make their own arrangements.

Royal apartments

A visitor of high rank in Tudor times would expect to pass through the Great Hall into the more exclusive rooms beyond. Similarly, a visitor in later centuries would climb the King's or Queen's Staircases to reach the State Apartments above. The sequence included a Guard Chamber; a Privy or Audience Chamber, where the king or queen sat beneath a Canopy of Estate; an eating room; an inner Privy Chamber; a Withdrawing Room; and finally a Bedchamber (figs. 4, 8 and 11). Here, select visitors were given privileged access: in the Withdrawing Room they were allowed to see the monarch in a less formal setting, perhaps to play games or for conversation. In the eighteenth century, the 'drawing room' became both a place and an event, an entertainment

7. Henry VIII dining in his Presence Chamber, alone at his table on a dais, surrounded by his court and served on bended knee. The figures on the left holding staves are the senior court officers, members of the King's Chamber.

with cards and tea-drinking where the king or queen would circulate for an hour or so.

With the passage of time the court became more formal both in terms of the variety of spaces it required and its personnel. Henry VIII's personal servants had been among the most powerful men in the land, as they controlled access to him and could speak to him in the most private moments. The Groom of the Stool was the most important courtier of all as he attended the king in the close-stool room (fig. 9). William III's own close stool (a chamber pot hidden under a padded seat) remains at Hampton Court Palace today (fig. 10).

By William's time, the state bed had become as much a symbol of power as was a throne. The later Stuart monarchs were heavily influenced by the ceremonies at the court of Louis XIV, the Sun King, in France, which included a *levée* (literally, getting up), the ceremony of dressing and undressing each morning and evening before members of the court and distinguished visitors. Despite the protocol, it was still possible to receive informal or secret visitors. On occasions when discretion was vital, visitors came in by the back stairs.

8. The King's Privy Chamber was the main ceremonial room in William III's palace. Ambassadors would approach the King seated beneath his Canopy of Estate, bow and kiss his hand. All palace ceremonial was focused on the monarch; courtiers would even be expected to bow to an empty throne as they passed.

9. (below) Hans Willem Bentinck, 1st Earl of Portland, the King's favourite, from the studio of Hyacinthe Rigaud, 1698–99. Bentinck was created Groom of the Stool to William III on 1 March 1689, but he fell from grace in 1700.

10. (bottom) This late seventeenth-century close stool, or portable toilet, was probably made for William III. The close stool gave its name to the king's chief officer and most intimate servant, the Groom of the Stool.

Courtiers' lodgings

In addition to the royal apartments, the palace always contained accommodation for courtiers. The house built for Cardinal Wolsey included Base Court, thirty suites of lodgings used for grand visitors. William III's courtiers squabbled over the allocation of lodgings in the newly rebuilt palace at the end of the seventeenth century. These suites of rooms, constantly altered, enlarged or squeezed, eventually became separate apartments used by the residents of the palace who were given permission to live there once the court no longer visited the palace.

The Story of Hampton Court Palace

From the sixteenth to the eighteenth centuries, life at Hampton Court was sleepy and rural between regular frenetic bouts of court residence, and also rebuilding works. In the course of 200 years the porters, cooks, guards, courtiers and monarchs themselves performed a complicated dance of ceremony. Life at court changed slowly over the centuries, becoming increasingly elaborate and formal but always remaining magnificent, until finally the court went and new inhabitants came. That history and those people are embedded in the fabric of the palace.

11. The elegance and formality of the court of William III reconstructed, in a modern photograph taken in the King's Guard Chamber. A hundred guards were appointed to attend the King, of whom forty would be on duty at any one time.

Life at Court

Before the Palace

Royal connections and evidence of great wealth at Hampton Court long pre-date the Tudor palace. The best-known home of the Tudor monarchs stands on a site that had been the scene of human activity for centuries. The bend of the River Thames as it snakes through the sands and gravel terraces below the Surrey hills provided a perfect location for an ancient settlement (fig. 12). The name 'Hampton' is Saxon – a settlement at the bend of the river. The area was certainly important in Anglo-Saxon times: King Athelstan was consecrated at nearby Kingston, the centre of a royal estate.

Domesday Book, the national land survey made for William the Conqueror in 1086, recorded that Sir Walter de St Valéry, a prominent Norman who had come over with the invasion forces, owned Hampton (fig. 13). By introducing sheep, St Valéry was able to build up a prosperous estate. The family was caught by the medieval passion for crusading to liberate the Christian sites in the Holy Land. Sir Walter took part in the First Crusade in 1096. In 1147–49 his grandson, Reginald, went on the Second Crusade, which succeeded in taking Jerusalem from the forces of Islam. In Jerusalem, medical treatment and hospitality were offered to visiting knights by a fighting order of monks, the Knights Hospitallers. Their original purpose was to nurse wounded crusaders, but in the late twelfth century the order was given permission to help defend crusaders' castle strongholds. Across Europe, regional priories raised money to be sent to the Grand Master (based in Rhodes from 1309 after Jerusalem had again fallen).

By the 1180s, Reginald's grandson, also Reginald de St Valéry, allowed the Knights Hospitallers to rent Hampton Court. From a document of 1338, we know that the house itself stood in an enclosure surrounded by a rectangular moat. There was probably a chamber block and a hall (traces of which have been found beneath the existing Great Hall), with a separate chapel to the east. The house was the centre of a large agricultural estate with 324 hectares (800 acres) of arable land and 2000 sheep. There was also a garden and a pigeon house, vital for providing fresh meat in the winter. A chamberlain, a baker, a gatekeeper and a chaplain assisted the permanent warden at the house. Hampton Court also served an important function as a guest house for visitors to the royal court when it was at nearby Byfleet.

12. (previous pages) Aerial view of Hampton Court from the west. In ancient times the confluence of the Thames with the lesser rivers of the Mole and the Ember made water transport easy. The plain was free-draining and fertile, if subject to occasional floods.

13. The record for the manor of Hampton in Domesday Book notes that the property had formerly been in the possession of Aelfgar, a Saxon earl. The manor of 1700 hectares (4200 acres) was valued at £39.

The Story of Hampton Court Palace

14. *The interior of Lord Daubeney's Great Kitchen. Completed dishes were passed through the hatch in the wall (far left) to the serving place beyond. Waiters then took them up to the waiting courtiers in the Great Hall.*

15. Daubeney's house
in about 1513, viewed
from the north-east, in a
reconstruction by Daphne
Ford. A moat surrounds the
site and the Great Kitchen
lies to the north (top right).

Later, the Knights Hospitallers found it more profitable to give their lease to secular owners. The first recorded lease was to John Wode, a favoured royal servant of Edward IV and Richard III. The Knights Hospitallers returned for ten years, before leasing Hampton Court to the courtier Giles Daubeney in 1494.

Lord Daubeney's Hampton Court

Giles, later Lord, Daubeney was one of Henry VII's staunchest supporters, and had spent a period of exile in France before Henry VII's accession. He fought bravely at the Battle of Bosworth in 1485, which was the closure of the dynastic Wars of the Roses with the death of Richard III in battle and the subsequent marriage of the Yorkist princess Elizabeth to the victorious Henry Tudor. In 1495 Daubeney became Lord Chamberlain of Henry VII's household. The guests he hoped to receive at Hampton Court were the sources of his power and privilege: the royal family. Daubeney tried to acquire the freehold to the manor, but got a ninety-nine-year lease from the Knights Hospitallers instead, with the right to 'take, alter, transpose, break, change, make and new build' the house according to his wishes. Daubeney took advantage of this to make great improvements to the manor, and some of his work still survives. His workmen completed a courtyard of dwellings, with a gatehouse to the west and a semi-detached kitchen to the north (fig. 16). This is the Great Kitchen that remains today, with an enormous fireplace for spit-roasts in its southern wall (fig. 14). Between the Great Kitchen and Great Hall, which stood side by side, was a serving-place from which the waiters took the dishes of food. A list from 1495 records that this Great Hall contained two fixed tables, two long trestle tables, four benches, a cupboard and a railing round the central hearth. Daubeney added a tower to the former chamber block, and according to the inventory the 'tower chamber' contained a press for clothes and a 'great coffer'. Today, an ancient bell

10 0   50   100   150

Feet

The Story of Hampton Court Palace

hangs above the inner gatehouse. Mentioned in a later lease of Hampton Court, it may be a survivor from the chapel of Daubeney's time or before.

This was a grand house, fit for entertaining royalty (fig. 15). The reserved and financially astute Henry occasionally used Hampton Court as a 'cell', or a retreat for periods of contemplation. On 7 January 1503 the Queen was rowed up the river from Richmond to the manor of Hampton Court in a 'great boat' for such a restful visit. Her servants kept the boat moored at Hampton Court for the week of her stay, which passed uncomfortably. Now in her mid-thirties, she was suffering from a difficult pregnancy, while only nine months previously she had learned that her eldest son, Arthur, Prince of Wales, had died in Ludlow. After leaving Hampton Court, the Queen was taken to the Palace of Westminster, where she and the King were to celebrate Candlemas together. On 2 February she gave birth prematurely to a daughter, Catherine, who lived only a few days. On 11 February the Queen herself died. Henry was bereft, but continued to visit Hampton Court until Daubeney's death in 1508 (fig. 17).

Henry himself died the following year. Hampton Court was soon to be transformed by its next two owners: the great Cardinal Wolsey and Henry VIII, Henry VII's surviving son. Under them it became the palace that is still familiar today.

16. *View into Clock Court, looking south from the roof of the Great Hall. The bricks set into the surface of the courtyard mark the position of Giles Daubeney's range (excavated in the 1960s and 1970s), which once stood here.*

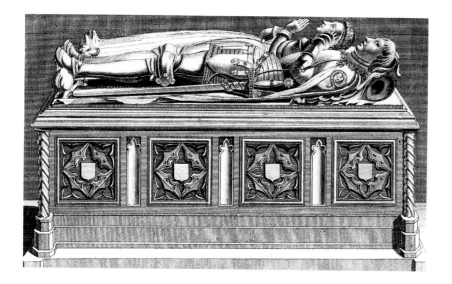

17. *The tomb of Giles Daubeney and his wife in Westminster Abbey. As a loyal courtier, Daubeney received many royal gifts; by the time of his death in 1508 he owned land in eight counties.*

Before the Palace

Cardinal Wolsey's Hampton Court Palace 1514–29

A terracotta panel set above Anne Boleyn's Gateway in Clock Court shows two cherubs holding up a coat of arms. Above them floats a wide-brimmed hat with many tassels (fig. 21). The arms and the hat – the ceremonial headgear of a cardinal of the Catholic Church – belonged to one of Hampton Court's most flamboyant owners, Thomas Wolsey (fig. 20).

Cardinal Wolsey was the last of his type. Great churchmen like him had been political leaders and prolific builders throughout medieval times, but Henry VIII took away much of this power by splitting the Church of England from the international church, refusing to recognize the authority of the Pope in Rome. Wolsey also had much in common with the princes of his own Renaissance times. He was interested in new artistic and cultural ideas, in the rediscovery of designs and ideas from Classical times, and in effective administration.

Thomas Wolsey was born in Ipswich, late in 1472 or early in 1473. His father, a butcher and grazier, was rich enough to send his son to the school of Magdalen College, Oxford. From there he was on the first rung of the ladder to high office. The Church was one of the few careers open to clever young men from non-aristocratic backgrounds, though the patronage of influential friends was important. One of Wolsey's supporters was the Archbishop of Canterbury, whose chaplain he became. By 1507 Wolsey had made the vital transfer to the King's household, becoming chaplain to Henry VII himself. As well as saying Mass, he had administrative tasks to perform and was sent on confidential missions abroad. Equally highly valued by Henry VIII, he received a clutch of bishoprics, and became Archbishop of York. By 1515 he was a cardinal, and in 1518 he became the Pope's legate in England.

Wolsey's enduring image is as a brooding and powerful figure, indeed as played by Orson Welles in *A Man for All Seasons* (fig. 19). In reality, we know relatively little about his appearance and character. His best-known biographer, George Cavendish, wrote after Wolsey's death to try to set the record straight. His talent for statecraft and his industry were prodigious: during negotiations with the French in 1527, Cavendish wrote, Wolsey worked from four o'clock in the morning until four o'clock in the afternoon, yet 'never rose once to piss, nor yet to any meat, but continually wrote his letters with his own hands, having all that time his nightcap and kerchief on his head'.

Wolsey's arch-critic the reformer William Tyndale gave him credit for being 'a gay finder out of new pastimes'. A prince of the Church needed to be able to entertain the great men of Europe. Once Wolsey

18. (previous pages) The inner face of Base Court, the principal surviving section of Cardinal Wolsey's palace; see fig. 23.

19. Cardinal Wolsey, as re-imagined by Orson Welles for the 1966 film A Man for All Seasons.

20. *Thomas, Cardinal Wolsey (1472/3–1530), by an unknown artist, late sixteenth century, from an original of c. 1520. Wolsey appears to be overweight in this portrait. He suffered from various ailments that match the symptoms of diabetes.*

CARDINAL WOOLSEY

21. After Wolsey's fall from grace, his arms in Clock Court, with their cardinal's hat and supporting cherubs, were covered up and replaced by the arms of Henry VIII. They were rediscovered only in the nineteenth century.

22. One of Giovanni da Maiano's eight roundels incorporating the heads of Roman emperors, executed in glazed terracotta. This is the head of Emperor Augustus.

23. The entrance courtyard, Base (or lower) Court. This view looking east shows Anne Boleyn's Gateway; the bell in the turret above may have belonged to Daubeney or the Knights Hospitallers. The courtyard's eighteenth-century network of cobbles and pathways was reinstated in 2009.

had become a cardinal, it was even possible that he could aspire to be the second English pope. Thomas More, Wolsey's successor as chancellor, described how Wolsey was glorious 'very far above all measure, and that was great pity; for it did harm and made him abuse many great gifts that God had given him'. To those writing afterwards, it seemed that Wolsey's great pride and success led inevitably to his terrible fall from power.

As Archbishop of York, Wolsey was entitled to York Place, his house in Westminster – later transformed by Henry VIII into Whitehall Palace. Hampton Court was the first house Wolsey acquired privately, and he did so because he needed an appropriately splendid country house for entertaining. He had probably met the previous owner, Giles Daubeney, at court. After Daubeney's death, his son was glad to pass the lease on to Wolsey in 1514 to clear his father's debts. Wolsey never managed to obtain the freehold of Hampton Court from the Knights Hospitallers; it fell to Henry VIII, the palace's next owner, to achieve this.

Wolsey's first phase of work, 1514–22

Wolsey quickly set repairs and improvements in hand. These were supervised by Lawrence Stubbs, a priest as well as the skilful administrator of Wolsey's building projects: the colleges he was building at Oxford and Ipswich, another country house at The More in Hertfordshire, and improvements to both Hampton Court and York Place. Wolsey's first phase of work at Hampton Court, built to the west of Daubeney's house, consisted of a whole new courtyard of accommodation, Base Court (fig. 23). Here, thirty pairs of rooms could be dressed with fine furniture and tapestries and allocated to guests who came from all over Europe to the Cardinal's palace (fig. 24). The plan of the rooms was innovative. Previously lodgings like this had garderobes in towers that protruded from their back walls; at Hampton Court the garderobes and chimneys

24. *(left) Reconstruction of a double lodging in Wolsey's Base Court, by Daphne Ford. A visitor arriving at Hampton Court entered his rooms from a covered walkway or gallery. He may have found his lodging decorated with tapestries from the Cardinal's collection, or he may even have brought his own hangings with him.*

25. *In 1771–73 Wolsey's Great Gatehouse was reduced in height from its original five storeys to three because of structural instability. This nineteenth-century reconstruction shows how it might have appeared in its original form.*

were built into the thickness of the walls between suites so that the building had a much neater appearance.

The entrance to Base Court was through the imposing Great Gatehouse, still the most instantly recognizable part of the whole palace. However, Wolsey would never have seen it in its current form, as it was altered at various times in the sixteenth century and in the eighteenth century its top two storeys were removed (fig. 25). Outside the gatehouse a large rectangular moat ditch was excavated for display rather than defence. Lost in subsequent years, the moat was re-excavated early in the twentieth century.

Wolsey added a daringly new long gallery, extending from the private chambers of Daubeney's house into the garden towards the south-east (the site of the Cartoon Gallery today). The gallery, 60 metres (200 ft) long, was used for exercise, conversation and viewing the gardens. It was especially innovative because of its Renaissance terracotta ornaments, incorporating the ancient Roman orders of architecture along with laurel wreaths. Another foreign and novel feature of Wolsey's palace was the series of roundels with heads of Roman emperors, made in glazed terracotta. Their Italian sculptor, Giovanni da Maiano, made eight busts for Hampton Court, using clay taken from the site itself (fig. 22). Although well known in Italy, this was a new style of decoration in England. It was wholly appropriate for a cardinal whose peers were the leading churchmen and princes of Renaissance Europe. Other lost elements in Wolsey's house, now known only from fragments, may have been designed to make this a most suitable house for a prince of the Church. Hampton Court was the first full flowering of the Renaissance in England.

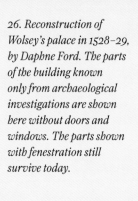

26. Reconstruction of Wolsey's palace in 1528–29, by Daphne Ford. The parts of the building known only from archaeological investigations are shown here without doors and windows. The parts shown with fenestration still survive today.

Wolsey's second phase of work, 1522–28

Wolsey's second phase of building took place in the six years from 1522 (fig. 26). Although no accounts survive for the work, we know that he improved the best chambers of the old house by creating three suites fit for royal occupation. The whole of the east side of Clock Court became a block of splendid royal lodgings, intended for Henry's daughter the Princess Mary on the ground floor, Henry VIII himself on the first floor and his first wife, Katherine of Aragon, on the second. In fact, the three of them could not have stayed at Hampton Court simultaneously, as the Princess had a household of 160 and the Queen of 200, and even Hampton Court could not have held all these people in addition to the King's own enormous winter household. The top-floor apartments were the most spectacular, for their windows were enormously high and wide, and would have amazed visitors passing through the gatehouse into Clock Court. Inside the apartments, grand stone doorways and fireplaces have survived subsequent alterations.

In 1526 Wolsey constructed a smaller but still luxurious suite for himself off a little courtyard to the south of Clock Court (fig. 29). His richly panelled rooms contained a decorative frieze made of leather mâché, a mixture of leather and glue moulded to form cherubs, vases and swirls (fig. 27). From his rooms, Wolsey looked out over sunny gardens to the south of the palace. To the south-west he had great fishponds constructed to provide fish for his table.

```
10  0      50      100      150
|--|--|--|--|--|--|--|--|--|
Feet
```

27. Fragments of the leather mâché frieze from Wolsey's new rooms of 1526. The design incorporated Renaissance cherubs and a classical vase.

Distinguishing this house from those of other courtiers were the Chapel and the grand processional route to it. In a king's or cardinal's household, the stately procession to chapel to hear Mass on feast days was an important ritual. Passing along the gallery, accompanied by his officers, the great man could see and be seen by the throngs of courtiers and visitors. At Hampton Court, Wolsey constructed a magnificent double-height chapel, with an enormous double window at its east end filled with stained glass (fig. 28). The gallery forming the royal route to the Chapel survives, known today as the Haunted Gallery. Beneath it ran a cloister for servants, giving access from courtyard to courtyard. Wolsey's chapel choir was excellent, so fine that in 1519 Henry VIII insisted that some of its members transfer to his own choir.

28. The east end of Wolsey's chapel was dominated by a great double window filled with stained glass designed by Erhard Schön from Nuremberg and including figures representing King Henry and Katherine of Aragon praying. This contemporary illustration of Henry VIII at prayer survives in the Tudor chapel at The Vyne, Hampshire.

29. Detail of the ribbed ceiling in Wolsey's rooms in the South Front of the palace, incorporating the Cardinal's badges. This is one of the most precious survivals of interior decoration from the Cardinal's palace. (The present ceiling includes new sections moulded from the original and made of fibreglass in 1961.)

30. *(below) The brickwork of the Tudor palace was adorned with 'diaper-work' black vitrified bricks laid in diagonal patterns. Vestiges of this survive in many parts of the palace walls.*

31. *(bottom) In this area of 'fictive' or false diaper-work decoration on the external east wall of the Chapel, the black pattern has simply been painted on to the bricks.*

Wolsey's Hampton Court was notable for the high quality of both materials and construction. Tudor bricks were by no means uniform in appearance, their colour and shape varying from batch to batch according to the clay and the maker. These differences are useful to today's archaeologists, who can identify the characteristics of a particular period. It is possible to work out that the royal lodgings, Wolsey's own lodgings and the Chapel were built in one campaign because they share similar bricks. The soft red brick of Wolsey's building was enhanced by patterns in 'diaper-work', diamond-shaped designs picked out in black or over-burnt bricks (fig. 30). This subtle decoration once covered most of the palace, although later repairs have erased or spoiled much of it (fig. 31).

One of the most sumptuous occasions at Wolsey's palace was the visit of the French ambassadors in 1527. Cavendish described the visit in great detail in order to record his former master's wealth and hospitality. In their sleeping chambers the French guests found silver vessels from which to drink and eat. Even their candles were extraordinary for the time, both white and yellow in three different sizes. Cavendish described the silver sconces lighting the dining room, probably what is now the Great Watching Chamber behind the Great Hall, the cupboard (literally a board for standing cups upon) holding gold and silver plates, the 'tall yeomen' standing by and, above all, Wolsey's spectacular tapestries. Wolsey's own closet was hung with cloth of gold, and he ended up with more than 600 tapestries in his collection.

Wolsey's fall

This kind of extravagance was expected from a great cardinal, but there were always people ready to criticize a churchman who spent so much on material possessions. One of these was John Skelton, who wrote in a biting satire that churches and cathedrals were falling down, while Wolsey spent his wealth on tapestry (fig. 32). Skelton even ventured on to the dangerous ground of comparing Wolsey's court to the King's:

> *Why come you not to Court?*
> *To which court?*
> *To the king's court?*
> *Or to Hampton Court?*
> *Nay, to the king's court!*

The king's court
Should have the excellence
But Hampton Court
Hath the pre-eminence!

Many have told the tale of how the proud cardinal made his house
unduly and dangerously magnificent, thereby offending the King, who
could not bear to be eclipsed. However, this is misleading. Wolsey's
great house was a *compliment*, not a threat, to the King. Henry had
always treated it as if it were his own. Wolsey's biographer recorded
that it often pleased the King 'to repair unto the Cardinal's house, as he
did diverse times in the year ... such pleasures were then devised for
the king's comfort and consolation as might be invented, or by man's
wit imagined'. Wolsey himself explained: 'I should have all this royalty,
because I represent the king's majesty's person in all the high courts
of this realm, to the terror and keeping down of all rebellious treasons,
traitors, all the wicked and corrupt members of this commonwealth.'

Wolsey was brought down not by Henry's envy but by the political
scandal of the King's 'great matter'. Like his royal master, Wolsey was to
suffer from the King's problems with his first wife.

*32. 'The Triumph of Fame
over Death', from a set of
tapestries depicting the*
Triumphs of Petrarch,
*woven in Flanders and
part of Wolsey's extensive
collection of tapestry. After
Wolsey's death, Henry VIII
took possession of it. This
was, and still is, hung in the
Great Watching Chamber.*

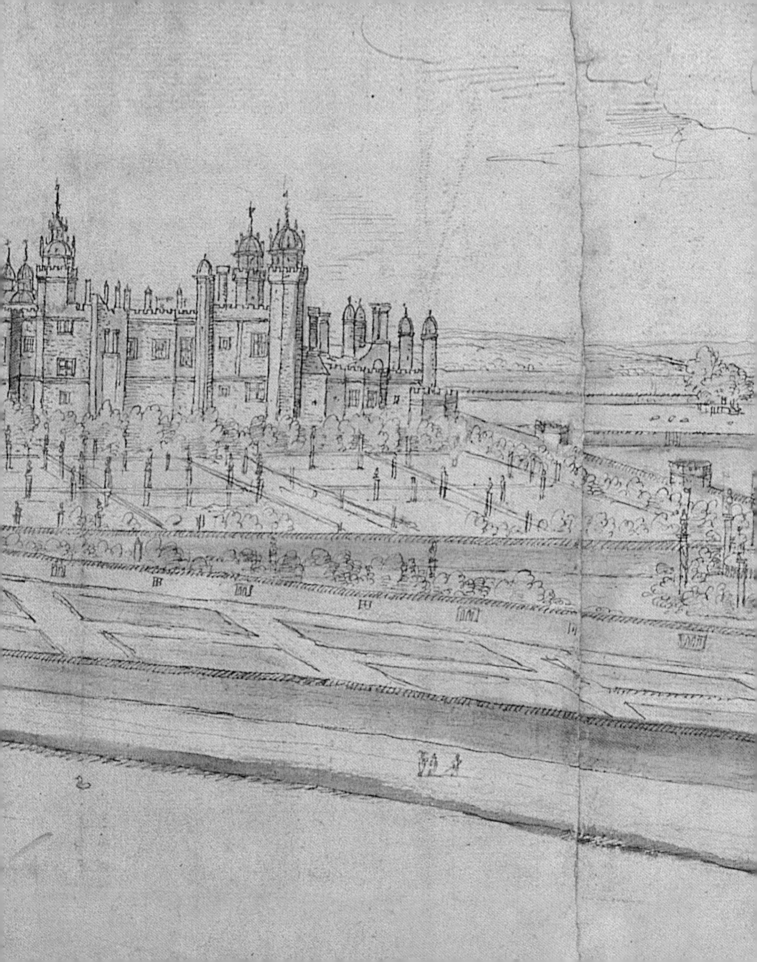

Henry VIII's Hampton Court Palace 1529–47

When Cardinal Wolsey wrote to Henry VIII (1509–47; fig. 35), he would address letters from 'your majesty's house' at Hampton Court. The convention was to speak as if the King owned each one of his subjects' houses, and it was an honour to them if he chose to stay there. Henry had visited Hampton Court throughout the 1520s, but Wolsey finally lost his sure political touch when he opposed the King's divorce from his first wife, Katherine of Aragon (fig. 34), and fell foul of the King's new mistress, Anne Boleyn (fig. 36). In September 1528 Wolsey received a peremptory letter from Henry's treasurer ordering him to vacate Hampton Court in four days' time. Henry had decided to eject Wolsey and to make Hampton Court his own.

Wolsey's difficulties were caused by Henry's decision to divorce Katherine, who had failed to provide him with a son. The King intended to marry Anne Boleyn, the courtier with whom he had fallen in love. A court of legates from Rome met to judge the matter but failed to agree and the case was called back to the Pope. This incident led to Henry's decision to separate the Church of England from that of Rome, with himself at its head. The move had far-reaching consequences, not least the dissolution of England's monasteries and a massive redistribution of their wealth. Wolsey appeared powerless to obtain the divorce the King wanted, and this confirmed Anne Boleyn as his bitter enemy. Even before Wolsey's fall from favour, work had begun on the construction of 'Anne Bouillayne's lodgynges at Hampton Courte'.

When news finally arrived that the Pope had categorically forbidden Henry's remarriage, Wolsey was disgraced. On 4 November 1530 he was arrested; falling ill with what was reported as dysentery, he died on 29 November. When Wolsey's servant George Cavendish brought the news to

34. *Katherine of Aragon, Henry VIII's first wife, whose failure to provide him with a living son and heir helped to precipitate the momentous political and religious change of the age.*

33. *(previous pages) Detail of Anthonis van den Wyngaerde's view of Hampton Court from the south, c. 1558–62; see fig. 47.*

35. Henry VIII, in a portrait after Hans Holbein. Despite his interest in building and his squirrel-like habit of collecting plate, jewellery and medals in the new Renaissance designs, the art that Henry loved most was music. Thirty-three of his own compositions have survived.

Henry VIII's Hampton Court Palace, 1529–47

Hampton Court, he found the King practising archery in the park and not over-eager to hear the news. 'I will make an end of my game,' Henry said, 'and then will I talk with you.'

Henry had not been greatly interested in architecture for the first twenty years of his life, leaving the necessary improvements to his palaces in Wolsey's hands. But now, with growing personal passion, he began to create a palace for pleasure and retirement with his second wife, Anne Boleyn, and his third, Jane Seymour (fig. 37), who had been Anne's lady-in-waiting. Both Anne and Jane had lavish lodgings built at Hampton Court, but ironically neither of them lived long enough to enjoy them. Anne Boleyn was beheaded on the grounds of treasonous infidelity, and Jane Seymour died shortly after she had successfully provided the King with a son and heir.

Henry VIII begins to build

Henry's programme of work began on 2 January 1529. The first phase of building included the construction of the enormous offices needed for Henry's kitchen staff, a Council Chamber from which he now intended to rule the country, and a tower of private rooms for himself. As many as 800 servants could accompany Henry on his visits to Hampton Court, and the kitchens he inherited from Lord Daubeney and Cardinal Wolsey were quite simply inadequate. In 1529–30 the capacity of the Great Kitchen to serve the meals eaten in the Great Hall was doubled and a second serving-place was added to the south, allowing twice as many waiters as before to carry food up to the Great Hall (fig. 43). The extended Great Kitchen contained six fireplaces. To its west three new small courtyards sprang up, surrounded by many specialized offices for boiling, pastry-making, fruit and spices. Confectioners worked in an upstairs room, producing delicate sweets and comfits on chafing dishes. There were larders for fish, meat and grain. The whole kitchen complex contained fifty rooms and three cellars. Officers of the Greencloth kept accounts; their office lay over the outer gate to the kitchens so that they could monitor supplies coming into the palace.

Given the number of people involved and the space constrictions, it is not surprising that frequent royal commands were needed to reform abuses. On one occasion the kitchen boys were commanded not

36. Anne Boleyn by an unknown artist, sixteenth century. The accusations against the King's second wife of adultery were almost certainly false. Her 'crimes' were failing to provide Henry with a male heir and her quarrel with the King's chief minister, Thomas Cromwell.

37. (opposite, top left) Jane Seymour, Henry VIII's third queen, gave him a son but died herself – at Hampton Court – in the process.

38. (opposite, bottom left) The 'Flanders Mare' Anne of Cleves, Henry VIII's fourth wife, was swiftly divorced as not being to his liking. She continued to live at Hampton Court as 'the king's sister'.

39. (opposite, right) Kateryn Parr, Henry VIII's sixth wife, outlived him; married four times herself, she was dead by her early thirties.

Henry VIII's Hampton Court Palace, 1529–47

40. (above) This detail of The Field of Cloth of Gold, *by an unknown artist, c. 1545, shows the temporary wooden palace surrounded by tents, and an octagonal wine fountain.*

41. *Chemical analysis of the contents of this chamberpot, excavated from the Tudor palace, shows that it still contains traces of urine.*

to 'go naked or in garments of such vileness as they do now, and have been accustomed to do, nor lie in the nights and days in the kitchen or ground by the fireside'. In 1554 a Spanish visitor to the court of Mary I described her kitchens as 'veritable hells, such is the stir and bustle in them ... The usual daily consumption is eighty to one hundred sheep ... a dozen fat beeves, a dozen and a half calves, without mentioning poultry, game, deer, boars and great numbers of rabbits. There is plenty of beer here, and they drink more than would fill the Valladolid river.'

Drinking water was brought to Hampton Court by a remarkable network of underground brick conduits and lead pipes running all the way from a spring on Kingston Hill. The sanitary needs of the throngs of Tudor courtiers were met in a variety of ways (fig. 41). The lodgings of senior members of the court, such as those in Base Court, had their own garderobe shafts. Lower-ranking members of the court would use the 'common jakes' in the south-west corner of the palace, later known as the Great House of Easement, where lavatories drained via the moat into the river. Fourteen people could be seated here simultaneously.

42. (left) Based on the wine fountain pictured in The Field of Cloth of Gold *painting (fig. 40),* this new wine fountain was installed in Base Court in 2010. By coincidence, the octagonal bases of fountains had been discovered in the archaeological investigation of Base Court (see fig. 201).

43. The office of the Clerk of the Kitchen, as re-presented in 2009. The clerks, whose office was located beside the serving hatches from which food was taken up to the Great Hall, recorded every dish as it passed before them.

Henry's second project was the creation of a Council Chamber, built just to the north-west of the Chapel, and a suite of private rooms for himself named the Bayne (or *bain*, bath) Tower (fig. 45). This new three-storey tower of lodgings lay to the east of Clock Court and contained a first-floor bedroom and adjoining bathroom. A furnace heated water for his circular bathtub. The first floor also contained his Privy Closet, decorated with Italianate wall paintings by Toto del Nunziata and with built-in cupboards. In Henry's library on the floor above, his books were protected behind lockable glass doors, with curtains to prevent fading. The first-floor bedchamber was the last in the chain of increasingly important rooms that extended from the palace entrance, eventually leading – for those who were sufficiently exalted – right to the King's own presence.

With so many people swarming around at court, there was little chance of maintaining order without the senior officers: the Lord Chamberlain and the Groom of the Stool. These two divided the governance of the King's lodgings between them, the Lord Chamberlain

Henry VIII's Hampton Court Palace, 1529–47

44. The Great Hall looking east. Sumptuously decorated, Henry VIII's Great Hall deliberately invoked medieval ideals of hospitality. Here the lesser members of the royal court ate dinner at royal expense in two sittings each day. The stained glass and the central door at the dais end are nineteenth-century embellishments.

The Story of Hampton Court Palace

being responsible for the outer rooms and the Groom of the Stool for the Privy Chamber and the private rooms beyond. Once Henry realized that these private or privy rooms were becoming less and less exclusive, he was motivated from 1537 to create the set of 'secret' lodgings that overlooked the gardens, in approximately the same position as the later suite of royal apartments built for William III. Henry's new lodgings formed the southern side of a new court, known as Cloister Green Court, roughly mirrored by the shape of today's Fountain Court, which replaced it more than 150 years later.

In 1532 Henry rebuilt the Great Hall (fig. 44), the first in the sequence of rooms leading towards his private lodgings. It seems that Wolsey himself had begun rebuilding Lord Daubeney's hall; the oriel window, for example, is almost identical to that constructed by Wolsey's masons at his Oxford college, Christ Church. It is not quite clear how far Wolsey's work had advanced, but this oriel window now became part of a dramatically improved Great Hall designed by Christopher Dickenson and James Nedeham.

The roof of the Great Hall is of hammerbeam construction. This design traditionally allowed carpenters to span halls of a greater width than the longest available timbers. In this case, timbers 12 metres (40 ft) in length, the width of the hall at Hampton Court, were readily available. The now archaic hammerbeam design, echoing the roof of Westminster Hall, was deliberately chosen to symbolize royalty, antiquity and chivalry. The roof was decorated with carved and painted heads, and badges celebrating the King and Queen. The carved screen that remains today was erected across the 'lower' or entrance end of the hall, supporting a gallery for musicians above, while a dais was constructed at the other, 'higher' end. An open stone hearth lay in the centre of the hall; yet the absence of any soot on the timbers of the shuttered louvre above it indicates that this equally archaic feature was probably never used.

As part of the rebuilding of the hall, a new processional staircase provided access from the gatehouse between Base and Clock Courts up to the first-floor level containing the hall and the King's lodgings. This entrance is called Anne Boleyn's Gateway today, and a new stone vault was constructed within it decorated with the initials of Anne Boleyn and Henry (replaced in the nineteenth century

45. The 'Bayne Tower' was begun in April 1529 to provide Henry VIII with a new suite of private rooms, including his great bath (or 'bayne') from which the tower derives its name.

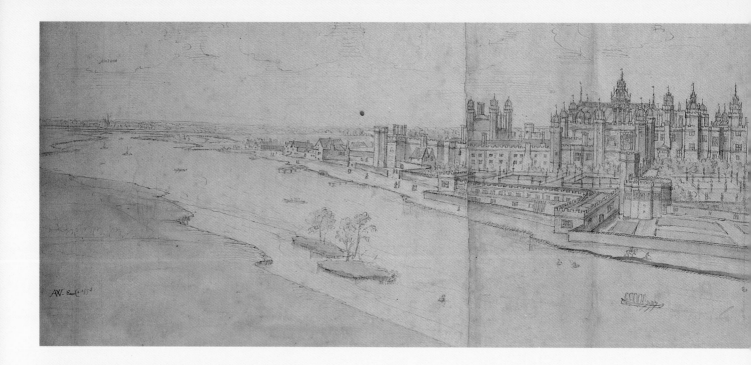

46. In 1533 craftsmen decorated the palace with the cyphers of Henry VIII and Anne Boleyn to celebrate their marriage. This nineteenth-century copy of their entwined initials decorates the vault beneath Anne Boleyn's Gateway.

with a copy of the original; fig. 46). Anne's badges and initials also appear next to Henry's beneath the royal coats of arms decorating the hall's roof. This was the busiest period of Henry's ten-year building programme at Hampton Court: 208 labourers, 45 carpenters, 70 masons and 81 bricklayers were employed at the palace in 1535.

The palace of pleasure

Henry and Anne regularly visited Hampton Court to inspect the progress of work and perhaps to enjoy some of the palace's amenities, which in due course would include extensive gardens (fig. 50), a tiltyard for jousting, archery butts in the park, bowling alleys and a workshop for the turner who made the King's bowling balls. Both outdoor and indoor tennis plays lay to the north-east of the palace (fig. 48). The Venetian ambassador described how Henry was 'most fond of tennis, at which game it is the prettiest thing in the world to see his play, his fair skin glowing through a shirt of the finest texture'.

Henry's Privy Garden lay to the south of the palace. Here heraldic beasts were mounted on poles, trellis fences created compartments in which plants were arranged in knot patterns, and a banqueting house with an onion-shaped domed roof stood on a mound reached by a spiral pathway. Down by the river, a large brick building, later known as the Water Gallery, was constructed upon piles (fig. 47). This provided a

convenient place for landing by boat as well as magnificent views
of the gardens and palace. The fishponds in the adjoining gardens
were kept full by the efforts of labourers who were paid for 'ladling
of water out of the Thames to fill the ponds in the night times'.

Hampton Court became a wonderful place for entertainment and
pleasure. In 1537 a dazzling display of the King's gold and silver plate
was set up in the banqueting house on the mound to impress onlookers.
Sir Thomas Cawarden's account books for 1546 record the construction
of a further two temporary banqueting houses in the park. Made of

*47. Anthonis van den
Wyngaerde's view of
Hampton Court from the
south, c. 1558–62. The
large building on the river's
edge is the Water Gallery,
where the royal barge
docked. Between it and the
palace lies Henry VIII's
magnificent Privy Garden,
with the King's heraldic
beasts on poles holding
gilded vanes.*

*48. This seventeenth-
century woodcut depicts a
game of tennis in a building
similar to Henry VIII's
covered tennis court, with
its roof and open sides that
could be closed by nets.
Henry also had an open
tennis court, probably on
the site of the seventeenth-
century structure that
survives today.*

49. (top) The Family of Henry VIII *by an unknown artist, c. 1545. Here Henry, his daughters Mary and Elizabeth, his wife Jane Seymour and their son Edward are all seen together. The scene is imaginary, as Jane died a few days after Edward was born. The royal family are shown in a rich Tudor interior similar to Henry's lodgings at Hampton Court.*

50. Based upon such sources as the painting The Family of Henry VIII *(fig. 49), a Tudor royal garden was established at Hampton Court in the Chapel Court in 2009–10, complete with hand-carved and painted heraldic beasts.*

waxed canvas with horn windows, they were intended for the reception of French visitors after the signing of a peace treaty. Henry also began to create a 4000-hectare (10,000-acre) chase, or private hunting ground, by seizing and fencing the surrounding land. The hunting available at Hampton Court was a considerable part of its appeal to the King, a keen huntsman, as were many of his successors.

Lodgings for Henry's queens

Katherine of Aragon had stayed in the suite of rooms built by Wolsey on the east side of Clock Court. Anne Boleyn had rooms at Hampton Court from 1529, but the old queen's residence was not good enough. Accordingly, in 1533 a grander suite of apartments was begun for her, forming the north and east sides of the new Cloister Green Court. Despite all this, in 1536 Anne fell from the King's favour. After giving birth to her daughter Elizabeth, and then miscarrying a boy, she was considered to have failed in her duty to provide the King with a male heir, and an excuse was found to accuse her of adultery, a treasonable offence for a queen. Meanwhile, Henry had been seen 'to affect Jane Seymour, and having her on his knee', which made Anne fear that he would cast her aside 'like the late queen'. Four months after the natural death of the repudiated Queen Katherine, Anne Boleyn was found guilty of treason and she bravely stepped on to the scaffold at the Tower of London, 'as gay as if she was not going to die'.

That very night Jane Seymour and the King dined together, and they were betrothed the next morning. With the King's marriage to Jane, a new flurry of work at Hampton Court began; the badges and initials of Anne Boleyn were erased and replaced by Jane Seymour's (figs. 51 and 53). Craftsmen received overtime payments for 'working in their own times and drinking times … for the hasty expedition' of the bridge over the moat where the leopard (Anne's symbol) was converted into Jane's panther (fig. 52). When Jane became pregnant the King's impatience was palpable. A great spurt of work was needed to provide bigger and better lodgings for the new Queen on the East Front. A further new set of lodgings for the prince that Jane was expected to provide was also begun on the north side of the palace. These contained a rocking room for the prince's cradle as well as his own Privy Kitchen.

In October 1537 the future King Edward VI was born at Hampton Court. Not quite two weeks later his mother died from complications following the birth, without ever having had the chance to take advantage of her new rooms and gallery looking east over the park.

Henry's fourth wife, the German princess Anne of Cleves, had little to do with Hampton Court as Henry, never satisfied with her physical appearance, soon divorced her (fig. 38). But the palace was the location of important scenes in the life of his penultimate wife, Catherine Howard (fig. 56). Henry's divorce from Anne of Cleves came through in July 1540. On 8 August Catherine Howard was married to Henry and, as the new Queen, sat next to him in the royal closet in the Chapel at Hampton Court. After making a progress round the country, they returned to Hampton Court on 24 October, and during Mass Henry gave 'most hearty thanks for the good life he led and trusted to lead with his wife'.

However, it was at Hampton Court little more than a year later that Catherine was first accused of the serious crimes that would lead to her being placed under house arrest and eventually condemned to death (fig. 54). Again the charge was

53. (right) The arms of Jane Seymour on a fragment of stone shield excavated from the moat in 1909–10. The design incorporates a phoenix, a hawthorn tree and a gateway.

51. (below) A roundel from the ceiling of the Great Watching Chamber, incorporating a Tudor rose. In 1536 John Hethe and Henry Blankston were paid for painting and gilding 130 leather mâché roundels on the ceiling of the Great Watching Chamber. The roundels were decorated with the badges of Henry VIII and Jane Seymour.

52. (bottom) The King's beasts guarding the moat bridge today are copies made in 1950 of an earlier set made in 1910, when the moat was excavated and the bridge restored. They include the Cadwallader dragon, the Clarence bull and the Beaufort greyhound, all celebrating the King's ancestry.

54. The Great Watching Chamber. Late in 1541, Catherine Howard's household were called here, told of the Queen's misdeeds, and dismissed from service. At that time there would have been a wide Tudor fireplace and a brightly coloured heraldic frieze between the tops of the tapestries and the ceiling.

55. The Haunted Gallery owes its name to the story of the desperate Catherine Howard. In the nineteenth century her ghost was described as 'a female form, dressed in white'. Residents living adjacent to the gallery reported 'unearthly shriek[s]' in the dead of night, 'followed immediately by perfect stillness'.

56. Portrait of Catherine Howard, Henry VIII's fifth wife. The King was described as being 'so amorous [of Catherine] that he knows not how to make sufficient demonstrations of his affection, and caresses her more than he did the others'.

adultery. She was accused of unchastity before she married, although it had been claimed that she came to Henry a virgin, but what sealed the Queen's fate was the rumour that during her marriage she had had an affair with Thomas Culpepper, one of the Gentlemen of the Bedchamber. Henry had been besotted with his new young wife and he turned against her all the more viciously.

The ghostly figure many claim to have glimpsed in the Haunted Gallery (fig. 55) is supposed to be Catherine herself, running along it in a desperate effort to reach the King at Mass to plead her innocence. There is no contemporary evidence for this; we do know that she was ordered to remain in her own rooms, and that she was allowed to keep her key to pass between her rooms, but from there she could not have reached the

gallery she is said to haunt. Catherine's pleas to her husband, wherever they were made, were of no avail: she was accused of leading 'an abominable, base, carnal, voluptuous, and vicious life, like a common harlot, with diverse persons' and was executed at the Tower of London on 13 February 1542.

The Chapel Royal

On religious feast days, the King would hear Mass from the Holyday Closet, a room overlooking the Chapel. On other days he was often keen to leave the palace early to reach the hunting field and would hear Mass at seven o'clock in his Privy Closet within his own lodgings, sometimes reading state papers throughout the service. On high feast days the King would process in a stately manner from his apartments to the Chapel, as Wolsey had done. The most important procession took place at Epiphany, the twelfth day of Christmas, for which Henry would wear his robes and crown (fig. 203).

The Holyday Closet and the Chapel itself were now far superior to the simpler structure that Wolsey had built. Henry's last great building project at the palace, the Chapel was begun in 1535. The most important change was the addition of the fantastical ceiling, which still survives (fig. 57). The designer was probably William Clement; the craftsmen John Hethe and Henry Blankston added colour and gilding. Like the Great Hall roof, the ceiling has many decorative flourishes: trusses, vaults, and pendant bosses decorated with angels blasting their trumpets. Its virtuosity clearly

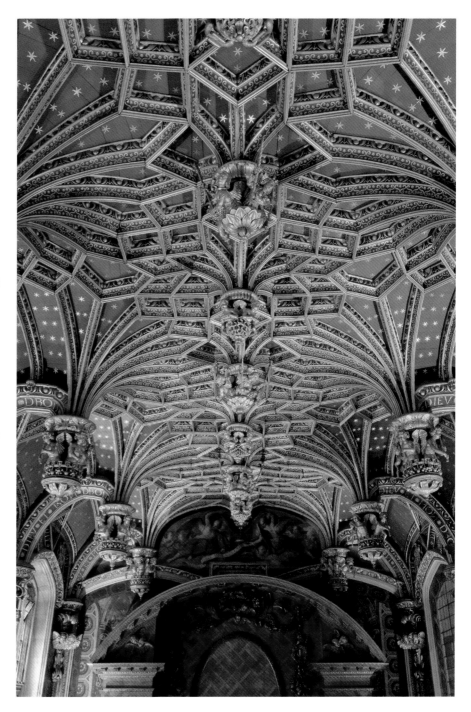

57. *The ceiling of the Chapel Royal was installed for Henry VIII in 1535–36. The ceiling's components were carved at Sonning, several miles further up the River Thames, before being transported to Hampton Court and reassembled there.*

demonstrates Clement's qualifications for his next task, to create another new palace for Henry not far from Hampton Court: the largely wooden structure of Nonsuch. Although little remains of Nonsuch Palace today, we can imagine its complexity and flamboyance from Hampton Court's Chapel ceiling. At the same time, the Royal Pew was refitted to create the Holyday Closet at the west end of the Chapel. Previously there had been one large room for the King's use; now two were created, with a painted screen incorporating stained glass separating the King's private pew from the Queen's. Here it was that Henry first received the fateful news of Catherine Howard's adultery.

Time and tide

One of the last additions that Henry made to the palace was the Astronomical Clock, which gives its name to Clock Court (fig. 58). Inscribed with the initials of its maker, Nicholas Oursian, and dated 1540, it has the earth at its pre-Copernican centre with the sun revolving around it, while outer dials show the movements of the moon and the number of days since the New Year. The clock's most cunning device was its ability to tell the time of high water at London Bridge, useful information at a period when tides governed travel to and from the palace.

With the proceeds from the Dissolution of the Monasteries, Henry VIII had become possibly the wealthiest monarch in English history. Hampton Court and his other palaces were refitted with the most sumptuous interiors, of which the distinctive group portrait of him with his children, of about 1545, gives a glimpse (fig. 49). The skyline was a fantasy forest of decorative chimneys, gilded domes,

58. The Astronomical Clock, made by Nicholas Oursian in 1540 to a design probably by Nicholas Kratzer, the astronomer described as 'Devisor of the King's Horologes'. Kratzer was paid fourpence a day in his post of Clock-keeper at Hampton Court.

The Story of Hampton Court Palace

vanes and heraldic beasts (figs. 33 and 59). Recent archaeology has uncovered evidence of two great fountains, on octagonal bases like those shown in the famous painting of the Field of Cloth of Gold held in 1520, which greeted visitors to Base Court (figs. 40 and 42). The glittering and bright Abraham tapestries still hanging in the Great Hall were the grandest of all the many fine tapestries in the palace, some from Wolsey's own magnificent collection, others like these acquired by Henry. In telling the story of Abraham, father of his people, Henry wanted people to make the connection with him and his Tudor dynasty, which would undoubtedly have as long and great a history (fig. 77).

After the death of Catherine Howard, the King aged rapidly, having 'wonderfully felt the case of the queen'. He grew increasingly fat – 'waxed heavy with sickness, age and corpulence of the body' – and lost the use of his ulcerated legs. However, he soon returned to Hampton Court, where he entertained the ambassadors from the Holy Roman Emperor Charles V,

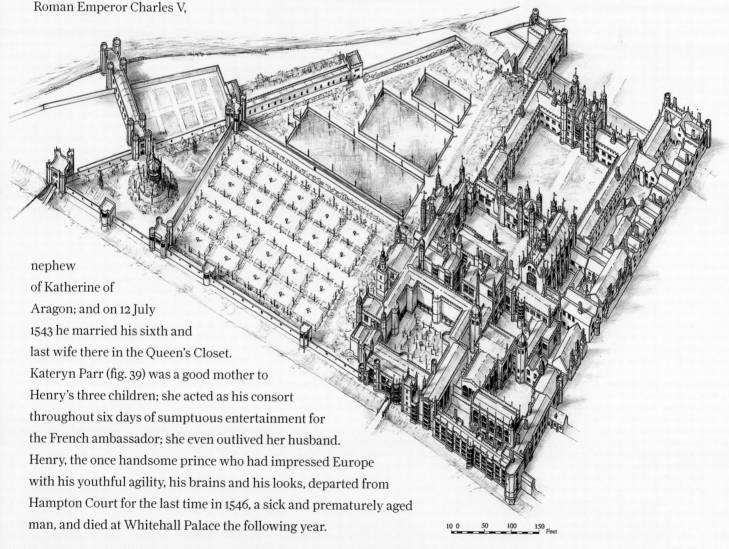

nephew of Katherine of Aragon; and on 12 July 1543 he married his sixth and last wife there in the Queen's Closet. Kateryn Parr (fig. 39) was a good mother to Henry's three children; she acted as his consort throughout six days of sumptuous entertainment for the French ambassador; she even outlived her husband. Henry, the once handsome prince who had impressed Europe with his youthful agility, his brains and his looks, departed from Hampton Court for the last time in 1546, a sick and prematurely aged man, and died at Whitehall Palace the following year.

59. Henry VIII's Hampton Court as it would have appeared in 1547, in a reconstruction by Daphne Ford. Some areas of the building are shown schematically because of the lack of evidence. Detail is provided for the areas that either survive today or are shown in historic views of the palace.

10 0   50   100   150 Feet

Henry VIII's Hampton Court Palace, 1529–47

Lifter

Uniral

Lonigin von Schotd.

Lestlan

The Later Tudors at Hampton Court Palace 1547–1603

Edward VI (1547–53)

Edward VI (fig. 62), born at Hampton Court Palace on 12 October 1537, entered the world in a bedchamber in the old queen's lodgings high up on the second floor of the east side of Clock Court. The new suite planned for his mother, Jane Seymour, was not completed in time. Jane did, however, benefit from new curtains and a new bed for the lying-in ceremony. It would turn out to be her deathbed only twelve days later.

With Edward's birth, Henry VIII's ambition to found a dynasty was achieved at last. A triumphant christening procession, one of the great set-piece occasions of the splendid Tudor court, was planned. On 15 October the procession began at the Prince's brand-new lodgings north of Chapel Court, passed through the adjacent Council Chamber, and snaked around the palace until finally arriving at the Chapel (fig. 61). Eighty knights, gentlemen and squires led the way, carrying wax torches that were to remain unlit until after the ceremony. Further noblemen and women carried the baby, with the train of his robe carefully fanned out behind him and a rich canopy held above him by Gentlemen of the King's Privy Chamber.

Edward's life was to be regrettably short. His father died when Edward was only nine years old, and the young Prince was placed under the care of his uncle, Jane's brother the Duke of Somerset, who declared himself the King's Protector. Hampton Court was a place that the boy King visited relatively frequently, often with his attendant gentlemen and his 'whipping boy' companion Barnaby FitzPatrick, to play games on horseback in the park or the Tiltyard. Somerset's custody of the young King was not well received by other nobles, and news came of a planned attack on Hampton Court to remove Edward from Somerset's influence. Armed men were drawn up and inspected in Base Court, but Somerset decided instead to flee with Edward to the safer stronghold of Windsor. It was all in vain: Edward fell ill – possibly with broncho-pneumonia – in February 1553 and died on 6 July at Greenwich, aged only fifteen.

60. (previous pages) Detail of Elizabeth I receiving Dutch emissaries, c. 1585; see fig. 65.

61. Part of the christening procession of Prince Edward, later Edward VI, in 1537. The baby Prince is carried beneath a canopy borne by gentlemen of the household. His elder half-sister Princess Mary follows him, with a lady-in-waiting carrying her train.

The Story of Hampton Court Palace

62. *Edward VI, from the studio of William Scrots, c. 1546. A constant companion of the young King was Barnaby FitzPatrick, with whom he shared his lessons. Barnaby was Edward's whipping boy; whether Barnaby or Edward misbehaved, it was always Barnaby who was chastised.*

Mary I (1553–58)

Edward's 'Device for the Succession', written on his deathbed, willed his crown to his Protestant cousin the Duchess of Suffolk. The Duchess's daughter, Lady Jane Grey, became queen for nine days before being deposed and executed by Edward's Catholic half-sister Mary, who as Henry VIII's eldest child had a much stronger claim to the crown.

The five years of Mary's reign were dangerous ones for England's Protestants, above all for the Queen's half-sister Elizabeth. Princess Elizabeth was next in line to the throne, but was imprisoned, accused of treason and even threatened with execution by Mary. Hampton Court Palace was the setting of many tense scenes.

In 1554 ambassadors arrived at Hampton Court to offer Mary the hand of the future King Philip II of Spain in marriage. After a ritual show of reluctance, she was pleased and seems to have become truly fond of her husband, despite his heavy Habsburg looks and gloomy temperament. Shortly after their marriage the thirty-eight-year-old Mary convinced herself that she was pregnant. In April 1555 the ladies of the court gathered at Hampton Court for the birth. Princess Elizabeth was brought to the palace and kept under close arrest – 'the doors being shut on her, the soldiers in their ancient posture of watch and guard' – for fear that she would lead a Protestant rebellion, but in the end Mary relented and freed her. On St George's Day Philip led a procession of the Knights of the Garter around the cloisters and courts. Mary peered down through her chamber window, so 'that hundreds did see her', in order to dispel rumours of her death before she could give birth.

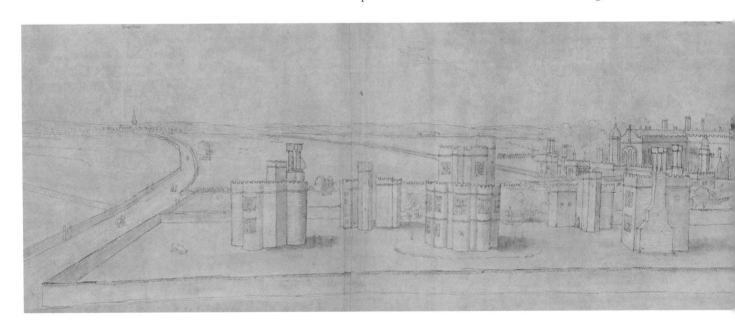

There was no baby. Mary's turned out to be a false pregnancy. In 1557 Philip returned to Spain, leaving Mary alone and childless, suffering from cancer of the stomach, which killed her in November 1558. Less than a week later the new Queen Elizabeth, aged twenty-five, entered London in triumph.

Elizabeth I (1558–1603)

When Elizabeth visited Hampton Court Palace she used her father's lodgings. She concentrated her building works on Whitehall Palace, but as early as 1559 the Lord Treasurer drew up a list of works required at Hampton Court. Although nothing would be done quickly, he wrote that he had 'found a new place for a privy kitchen and all offices to it' with the advantage that 'the trouble of the old privy kitchen and the sewers of all evil savours from the same shall be clearly taken away'. This was the private kitchen where Henry VIII's own meals had been cooked. In 1570 a new Privy Kitchen was built, and it still stands, to the east of Daubeney's kitchen.

Other improvements were made at the same time to the southern side of the palace, and the walls there bear the Queen's monogram and date (fig. 64). By blocking the windows on to the ponds area to the south, Elizabeth could 'walk secretly all hours and times without looking upon her out of any place'. On cold mornings she liked to march about vigorously in the gardens. Only if onlookers approached would she adopt a slower and more regal pace. Elizabeth appointed the Frenchman John Markye to carry out improvements to the privy

64. Elizabeth's initials and the date 1568 are displayed on a bay window that was added to the South Front of the palace during her reign.

gardens, replacing the many elaborate compartments with larger divisions in which the Queen's badges were set out in coloured gravel.

Elizabeth had first returned to Hampton Court as queen nine months into her reign (fig. 65). She was at the palace once again in October 1562, and nearly lost her life. She was so ill with smallpox that her doctors thought she could not recover, but by the end of the month she was out of bed, and 'attending to the marks of her face to avoid disfigurement'. However, the disease caused the death of Sibell Penn, a lady of Elizabeth's bedchamber and Edward VI's former dry-nurse. Mrs Penn's death gives rise to one of the most persistent ghost stories of the palace: her unquiet spirit is said to have been heard turning a spinning-wheel in the palace after her tomb in Hampton parish church was disturbed in 1829.

After her bout of smallpox, Elizabeth kept away from Hampton Court for five years. Only from 1567 did it once again become a regular autumn or winter residence. In December 1568 the Casket Letters incriminating Mary Queen of Scots were produced to the great council of peers assembled there. The palace's regular entertainments included tilting (fig. 66) or jousting, especially on the Accession Day. Henry VIII's viewing towers overlooking the lists in the Tiltyard (fig. 63) may not actually have been used in his time, but in 1569 they housed spectators at the first tournament of Elizabeth's reign to be held at Hampton Court. At Christmas and New Year, the Great Hall of the palace was transformed into a 'masking house' or indoor theatre and became the setting for masques and plays. A stage was erected, the Great Watching Chamber was used for rehearsals and the pantry behind the screens passage became the 'tiring' or dressing room for the actors. Painted canvas backdrops included views of 'seven cities, one village, and one country house'.

The marvels of Elizabeth's palace included the fabulous room to

the south-east called 'Paradise'. Built by
Henry VIII, it was now refurbished with
a new painted ceiling and decorated with
precious metals and gems. Visitors found
that 'everything glitters so with silver, gold
and jewels, as to dazzle one's eyes, there is a
musical instrument made all of glass except
the strings'. Here the Queen entertained her
most distinguished guests and her greatest
favourites. Among those favourites were
Robert Dudley, whose apartments were
controversially moved close to hers, and
Walter Ralegh. He brought with him in
October 1584 some of the strangest visitors the
royal palace had ever seen, the first two Native
Americans to come to England from his New
World colony at Roanoke in Virginia (fig. 67). 'They wear no shirts',
the visitor Lupold von Wedel wrote, although to meet the Queen, for
modesty, 'they are clad in brown taffeta'.

One of the last improvements to Elizabeth's palace, between 1584
and 1591, was a replacement for her father's great fountain in what is
now Clock Court. The earlier Gothic fountain may have been wooden
and have rotted away. The new octagonal design with classical details
contained a secret waterworks
that would spray the unwary.

Elizabeth had other secrets;
rooms for practising alchemy to
find the philosopher's stone that
would turn base metal into gold
and give her eternal life. She
failed, and died at Richmond
Palace on 24 March 1603.

66. A Tudor tiltyard
in action. The judges
watch from an elaborate
three-storey building
situated inside the lists.
Elizabeth I enjoyed
watching and taking
part in sports.

67. Natives from
Sir Walter Ralegh's ill-fated
Roanoke colony in North
America were among the
most exotic visitors to the
court of Elizabeth I. This
watercolour of a shaman
from the Roanoke people
was painted by John White,
the colony's governor.

The Later Tudors at Hampton Court Palace, 1547–1603

Seventeenth-Century Hampton Court Palace 1603–89

James I (1603–25)

A new king and a new dynasty as well as a new century arrived with the accession of Elizabeth's Scottish cousin to the throne of England in 1603 (fig. 69). The Protestant James VI of Scots, son of the Catholic Mary Queen of Scots who had been the focus of many plots against Elizabeth, came to London with a new band of courtiers and a new style of culture and entertainment.

Bubonic plague raging in London drove the court to celebrate the first Christmas and New Year of James's reign at Hampton Court. 'The Queene intendeth to make a mask this Christmas', announced the King's cousin Arbella Stuart in a letter written from the palace, and permission was given for the late Queen Elizabeth's wardrobe at the Tower of London to be raided for costumes (figs. 71 and 72). In Samuel Daniel's masque *The Vision of the Twelve Goddesses*, the Queen herself took 'the part of Pallas, in a blue mantle, with a silver embroidery of all weapons and engines of war, with a helmet-dressing on her head', and she performed a dance before the King seated in the Great Hall beneath his Cloth of Estate (fig. 70). Ambassadors and courtiers joined in the dancing, and young Prince Henry was thrown between them 'like a tennis ball'.

One hostile but influential observer described how the new King was 'of middle stature, more corpulent through his clothes than his body' (he wore padded doublets to protect him from an assassin's dagger) and

his eyes were 'large, ever rolling after any stranger that came in his presence'. His tongue was 'too large for his mouth, which ever made him speak full in the mouth and made him drink very uncomely'. This well-known, unkind pen-portrait masks a bisexual, intelligent and disputatious monarch, whose time at Hampton Court was characterized by his

68. (previous pages) Hendrick Danckerts, Hampton Court Palace (detail), c. 1665–67. This view of the palace from the east was probably painted to record Charles II's newly dug Long Water Canal and the avenues of lime trees.

69. James I, after John de Critz the Elder, c. 1606. The only son of Mary Queen of Scots, James was a successful king of Scotland and was invited to take the English throne as well after Elizabeth I's death in 1603. He was witty and scholarly, although sometimes brutally frank to those who opposed him.

The Story of Hampton Court Palace

love of literature as well as of lavish entertainment. The early Stuart court was notorious for the inventiveness of its masques and for its debauchery. Performances were followed by a rush to supper in the King's Presence Chamber, where courtiers seized food and drink with 'accustomed confusion'. Visits from the Danish family of James's wife, Anne, were particularly riotous.

Yet Hampton Court was not all frivolity. The celebrations in the Great Hall for the New Year in 1604 included performances by the

King's Men, whose resident dramatist was William Shakespeare. *Hamlet* and *Macbeth* were probably among the plays performed. Later that same month came James I's great religious conference at Hampton Court.

The King invited representatives of the radical puritan movement and the more conformist members of the Church of England to discuss their differences over doctrinal issues, such as the place of bishops and ritual in worship. The meeting led to the decision to publish an authorized translation of the Bible into English, the King James Bible.

The members of the delegation of the acceptable face of puritanism, led by Laurence Chaderton (fig. 73), Master of Emmanuel College, Cambridge, were permitted to enter the Privy Chamber, where 'kneeling, they made their case to the King, who was seated with the young Prince Henry on a stool at his side', but the King disregarded and disdained their arguments. 'No bishop, no king' was his mantra, and James joined in theological debate himself, though Sir John Harington recorded that he 'disputed with Dr Reynolds [a puritan]; but he rather used upbraidings than arguments; and told them they wanted to strip Christ again, and bid them *away with their snivelling*'.

James's other great passion – apart from young men such as his favourites Robert Carr, Earl of Somerset, and George Villiers, Duke of Buckingham – was hunting. He restocked the park and Hampton Court

71. *Marcus Gheeraerts the Younger,* Portrait of an Unknown Woman, c. 1590–1600. *This lady's unusual and highly decorative costume – possibly intended to be Persian – suggests that she is dressed for an Elizabethan or Jacobean court masque.*

72. *Gerrit van Honthorst,* Mercury Presenting the Liberal Arts to Apollo and Diana, 1628. *Charles I and Henrietta Maria (left) are depicted as Apollo and Diana. The Duke of Buckingham below is Mercury in his winged cap. Masques and allegory were an important component of life and entertainment at the early Stuart court.*

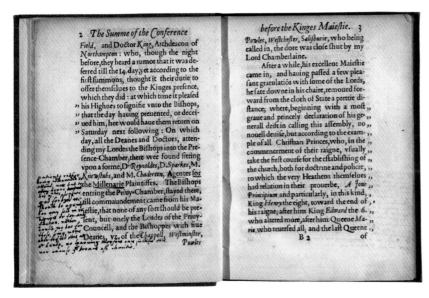

2 *The Summe of the Conference*
Field, and Doctor *King*, Archdeacon of *Northampton*: who, though the night before, they heard a rumor that it was deferred till the 14. day, yet according to the first summons, thought it their dutie to offer themselues to the Kinges presence, which they did: at which time it pleased his Highnes to signifie vnto the Bishops, that the day hauing preuented, or deceiued him, hee would haue them return on Saturday next following: On which day, all the Deanes and Doctors, attending my Lordes the Bishops into the Presence-Chamber, there wee found sitting vpon a forme, D. *Reynoldes*, D. *Sparkes*, M. *Knewstubs*, and M. *Chaderton*, Agentes for the Millenarie Plaintiffes. The Bishops entring the Priuy-Chamber, stayed there, till commaundement came from his Maiestie, that none of any sort should be present, but onely the Lordes of the Priuy-Councell, and the Bishoppes with fiue Deanes, viz. of the Chappell, *Westminster*, *Powles*

before the Kinges Maiestie. 3
Powles, *Westchester*, *Salisburie*, who being called in, the dore was close shut by my Lord Chamberlaine.

After a while, his excellent Maiestie came in, and hauing passed a few pleasant gratulatiõs with some of the Lords, he sate downe in his chaire, remoued forward from the cloth of State a prettie distance; where, beginning with a most graue and princely declaration of his generall drift in calling this assembly, no nouell deuise, but according to the example of all Christian Princes, who, in the commencement of their raigne, vsually take the first course for the establishing of the church, both for doctrine and policie, to which the very Heathens themselues had relation in their prouerbe, *A Ioue Principium* and particularly, in this kind, King *Henry* the eight, toward the end of his raigne; after him King *Edward* the 6. who altered more, after him Queene *Marie*, who reuersed all, and the last Queene B 2 of

73. *(left) The semi-official account of the Hampton Court Conference of 1604 by William Barlow was sharply contradicted by Laurence Chaderton, leader of the puritan contingent, in this marginal note in his own hand.*

74. *The Horn Room was originally a waiting area for servants bringing food up from the kitchens below. In the seventeenth century the horns were displayed in the Tudor Queen's Gallery on the east side of the palace, which eventually became known as the 'Horne Gallery' as a result.*

became a useful base for his sport. Some of the wooden stags' heads mounted with antlers that remain in the Great Hall and Horn Room date from Stuart times (fig. 74).

Under James I, Hampton Court benefited from a low but continuing level of expenditure on maintenance. The Great Hall was repaired in 1614, the Astronomical Clock was repainted in 1619, and the ceiling of the Paradise Chamber underwent lengthy restoration. The royal court fell into the pattern of an annual autumnal visit to the palace, but it was home for longer periods to James's eldest son, Henry, Prince of Wales. He died on 6 November 1612, aged only eighteen. His mother, Queen Anne, was at Hampton Court when she too died in 1619. One of her ladies recorded how 'we all stayed in the chamber next to her bedchamber till she sent a command

75. *The tennis court, built
in the reign of Charles I
and remodelled in the reign
of Charles II, is still in use
today and is the venue
for the British Open Real
Tennis Championships. The
game is played by bouncing
the ball from the roofs of the
penthouses surrounding the
court, as well as passing it
over the net.*

to us to go to bed, and would not suffer us to watch that night'. At the last, the Queen 'had the pleasantest going out of this world that ever anybody had'.

Charles I (1625–49)

At the time of his accession in 1625, Charles I was heavily influenced by his father's former favourite, the Duke of Buckingham. The Duke took a flattering interest in the shy and stuttering Charles, seriously rivalling his new wife, the French princess Henrietta Maria, in the King's affections. Hampton Court became the setting for painful quarrels between Queen and King; one of the points at issue was the Queen's large, French-speaking household. The French ambassador, arriving in

England in the hope of making peace between the royal couple, paid a visit to Charles I at Hampton Court and was received in a gallery. Charles raged at his wife's refusal to embrace English ways, or even to learn the English language. To the ambassador's annoyance, the Duke of Buckingham interrupted this painful private audience.

Charles made several important additions to the palace. The first, carried out in the autumn of the first year of his reign, was the building of a new tennis court (fig. 75). The rules of the game had changed since the time of Henry VIII; his open tennis play, on the same site as the present Royal Tennis Court, was replaced in stone. The heraldic Privy Garden was replaced by a simpler layout of four quarters in lawn, with statuary and sundials. The canalized Longford River, which cost over £4000 to construct in 1638–39, still brings water from 18 kilometres (11 miles) away to power the fountains of the palace gardens. The Tudor conduits providing drinking water from a spring on Kingston Hill were overhauled at the same time.

At Hampton Court Charles I arranged and maintained the contents of the palace according to old-fashioned principles. The inventory of his goods made for Parliament in 1649 after his execution shows that there were over 250 tapestries at Hampton Court, many of which had survived from the previous century. The late-Henrician set telling the story of Abraham (fig. 77) was now worth an astonishing £8260.

76. (left) Andrea Mantegna, Triumphs of Caesar, *Canvas II: 'Bearers of statues of gods, of an image of a captured city, siege engines, inscribed tablets and trophies'.*
The series of Triumphs paintings was considered important enough to be kept behind when the contents of Hampton Court were put up for sale during the Commonwealth.

77. *'The Circumcision of Isaac' from* The History of Abraham *series of tapestries, c. 1545. Acquired by Henry VIII and intended for the Great Hall, the tapestries telling the story of Abraham remained in the Stuart palace. The birth of Isaac, heir to the aged Abraham, had both personal and dynastic significance for Henry VIII.*

78. A detailed survey of Hampton Court from the east, dating from between c. 1656 and 1670. From left to right: the towers on the wall of the Privy Garden, the turrets of Henry VIII's private lodgings, the end of the Great Hall, the Queen's lodgings and the tennis court.

Elsewhere in the palace, Henry VIII's purple velvet canopy of state decorated with agates, chrysolites, garnets, sapphires and a large pearl was still in use, as were four great state beds from his day. Charles I was himself the greatest art collector among all British monarchs. His appetite for collecting was vast. Living among these antique furnishings, Charles I selected appropriate paintings to complement them, mainly portraits or religious subjects. His most striking new addition was Andrea Mantegna's series of the *Triumphs of Caesar* (fig. 76), purchased from the Gonzaga family in Mantua together with many other paintings from their celebrated collection. The *Triumphs* paintings arrived in England in 1630 and were installed in the Tudor long gallery. Calico curtains protected them from the light; today they may still be seen, in darkened conditions, in the Lower Orangery.

The Civil War and Commonwealth (1649–60)

From the 1630s onwards Charles I was in a difficult position: he needed money but had been unable to convince the Lords and Commons that he deserved it, so he ruled without summoning Parliament, raising money through a variety of expedients. Relations between king and country deteriorated until both sides eventually resorted to arms, and in 1643 Parliamentarian forces seized Hampton Court. They removed all the fine fittings from the Chapel: 'the Altar was taken down ... the Rails pulled down, and the steps levelled; and the Popish pictures and superstitious Images that were in the glass windows were also demolished'. Only the elaborate ceiling remained above a white-painted room for preaching, with twelve long hard forms laid out for the congregation.

By 1647 Charles I had lost a series of vital battles against the Parliamentarians and Hampton Court was selected as the captured King's prison. Oliver Cromwell (fig. 79), leader of the opposing forces, permitted the King to lead an elegant and comfortable life at the palace,

The Story of Hampton Court Palace

more 'as a guarded and attended prince than as a conquered and purchased captive'. During his imprisonment, Charles was allowed visitors, including his children and the loyal John Evelyn, who kissed the King's hand and described his captors as 'execrable villains'. Even Cromwell paid visits to the King, in the hope of reaching some kind of compromise. He regretted the laxity of the prisoner's regime when in November Charles managed to escape.

Attendants told Colonel Whalley, who was in charge of the King's security, that their master was writing letters in his bedchamber. He recalled that by six o'clock 'I began to doubt, and told the bed-chambermen, Mr Maule and Mr Murray, I wondered the king was so long a-writing.' Suspicious, Whalley 'lookt oft in at the key hole to see whether [he] could perceive his majesty, but could not', so at eight o'clock he demanded access through the back and found the bedchamber empty. The bird had flown; Charles had escaped across the garden to be carried away in a waiting boat. Within two years he would be recaptured and executed in front of his own palace of Whitehall.

Parliamentary Commissioners were responsible for the fate of the palace. It was decided that Oliver Cromwell, leader of the newly founded Commonwealth, would himself require a country house. While some items from the furnishings at Hampton Court were retained for the Commonwealth's use, many items were lost or sold. A visitor in 1652 reported that the only tapestries left at Hampton Court were the ones 'which had been behind the good ones to protect them from the damp of the walls'. By 1653 Cromwell had been made Lord Protector, reigning almost as a king. Whitehall was his principal residence, but he spent most weekends at Hampton Court. 'His custom', his biographer James Heath recorded, 'was now to divert himself frequently at *Hampton Court* (which he had saved from Sale, with other Houses of the King's, for his own greatness), whither he went and came in post, with his Guards behind and before, as not yet secure of his Life from the justice of some avenging hand'. He was right to be cautious:

79. *Oliver Cromwell, miniature by Samuel Cooper, c. 1650. In 1628 Cromwell experienced the dramatic religious conversion that motivated him throughout the rest of his life as a revolutionary. He was perennially troubled by malarial fevers, and one of these triggered the chest infection and pneumonia that killed him in 1658.*

Charles I's son, now in exile, promised a reward to anyone who would assassinate Cromwell. In fact, Captain Thomas Gardiner later petitioned Charles II for money, which he claimed he deserved for his unsuccessful attempt on Cromwell's life in a gallery at Hampton Court.

In some senses Cromwell did not act like a king. He commanded Sir Peter Lely to make his portrait 'truly like me, and not flatter me at all; but remark all these roughnesses, pimples, warts and everything'. He kept open house at Hampton Court for the officers of the army, dining with them himself, when he would 'disport himself, taking of his Drink freely, and opening himself every way to the most free familiarity'. Yet this inspired soldier and religious extremist adopted many of the trappings of the royal family that he had toppled. His 'Rich Bedchamber' in the Queen's Apartments, for state rather than sleeping, was hung with five tapestries telling the story of Vulcan and Venus; his couch, two 'elbow chairs' and four 'back stools' there were covered in 'sky collour damaske'.

Cromwell brought the delicate mythological figure of Arethusa from Somerset House to add to the central fountain of the Privy Garden; the statue was by Hubert Le Sueur, an artist indelibly associated with the deposed Stuart regime. Cromwell's more puritanical supporters criticized him for having such titillating statues in the Privy Garden. Surrounded by her boys and dolphins, Arethusa stayed, although she would later be moved again, this time to Bushy Park, near the palace (fig. 80). Renamed Diana, she stands at the centre of a grand eighteenth-century landscaping scheme.

Charles II (1660–85)

After Cromwell's death in 1658, his son Richard attempted briefly and unsuccessfully to take up the reins of power. The country decided that it preferred the house of Stuart, and Charles II was invited to return to his father's throne (fig. 83). Witty as always, the cynical King asked the crowds of courtiers clustering round to welcome him home to Whitehall in 1660 why he had been in exile for so long, 'for I see nobody that does not protest he has ever wished for my return'. Charles II was a frequent visitor to Hampton Court, coming first in the month he was restored to the throne. The palace was the setting for some of the amorous adventures for which he is best known. As he had spent so many years in the licentious court of France, he found himself criticized back in England for his easy relations with women and the attention he paid to

80. The fountain of Arethusa (now known as Diana) in Bushy Park today. It was moved here from the Privy Garden in 1714.

The Story of Hampton Court Palace

their views. His household ordinances demanded a strict standard of behaviour that the King himself did not always match.

One of the King's many mistresses, Barbara Villiers, Countess of Castlemaine, was installed at Hampton Court, where she lived with the illegitimate children she had by him, and was given the lucrative office of Keeper and Chief Steward of the Mansion and Honour of Hampton Court. Lady Castlemaine is one of the beauties of Charles II's court painted by Sir Peter Lely in a series of portraits hanging today in the Communication Gallery (figs. 81 and 82). The idea for the portraits came from the King's sister-in-law Anne Hyde, Duchess of York, who was 'desirous of the Pictures of the most handsome Persons about the Court', herself included.

The King's mistresses frequently presented Charles's wife, Catherine of Braganza, with a difficult situation, not least when she was expected to receive them at court. Catherine, not herself a great beauty, had come to England from Portugal in 1662. The artist and poet William Schellinks witnessed the often-chaotic preparations made for her honeymoon at Hampton Court, including the provision of a great green velvet bed topped with plumes. The Queen's lodgings were redecorated and a private Catholic oratory was set up for her. On 29 May, the King and his new Queen arrived by coach. The aristocracy of England lined up to greet them, and the new Queen walked through

81. (above) Barbara Villiers, Countess of Castlemaine by Sir Peter Lely, c. 1665, from Lely's series of beauties of the Stuart court. In 1663 it was said that she 'commands the King as much as ever'. In about 1671 she lost her place as Charles II's chief mistress to Louise de Kéroualle, Duchess of Portsmouth.

82. The Communication Gallery is hung with a series of portraits painted by Sir Peter Lely between c. 1662 and 1665, known as the 'Windsor Beauties'. They represent the most beautiful women at the court of Charles II.

each room, acknowledging nobles of ever-higher rank before finally reaching her own bedchamber on the East Front.

Money was a perennial problem for Charles II. On his return from exile he had revived the hospitable custom of providing meals for the whole court, but the royal purse could not bear the expense. Outcry accompanied the abolition of free meals for lower courtiers in 1662. In 1664 the royal household's staff was reduced from 225 to 147. The Great Kitchen, no longer required for mass catering, began to be split up for individual courtiers' cooks, and the courtiers ate their meals in small groups in one another's lodgings. Otherwise, throughout the seventeenth century, Hampton Court saw remarkably few changes or improvements. By and large, the Stuarts kept the palace as a monument to their Tudor forebears, 'a relic of departed greatness' as the Venetian ambassador remarked in 1653.

83. *Charles II by John Michael Wright, c. 1661–62. Although many of the changes to the palace building made by him or the Countess of Castlemaine, his one-time mistress, were swept away before the end of the century, Charles II left an enduring mark in the form of the park landscape.*

However, Charles did make several significant improvements. One of these was the refurbishment of Charles I's tennis court to make the structure that still survives. The lines on the court were laid out in black marble, and the workmen were paid for the necessary building works. The King also spent leisure hours on a new bowling green by the river, constructed in 1670. The Count of Grammont reported how, 'As soon as the heat of the day is over, the company assemble there: they play deep: and spectators are at liberty to make what bets they please.'

The other major changes made by Charles II were the conversion of the old Tudor tennis court east of Chapel Court into lodgings for his brother, the Duke of York, and the construction of his own new lodgings

The Story of Hampton Court Palace

in the south-east corner of the palace. This brand-new building, described as 'Next Paradise' because of its proximity to the Tudor Paradise Chamber, had only a short life, as it was to be demolished in the next reign (fig. 84). Constructed in rubbed red brick, it provided a neat block of modern lodgings for Charles. In 1675 the boards across the opening from Henry VIII's lodgings into the new rooms were removed, and the King slept in his new block while staying at Hampton Court for council meetings that summer. These rooms faced east towards the park, where Charles II's improvements were even more striking. In preparation for the arrival of Catherine of Braganza, the magnificent Long Water Canal was cut through the park and 758 Dutch limes were planted in avenues along its flanks (fig. 68). William Schellinks described how one could glide 'by water with the barges right up to the gardens'.

James II (1685–88)

Charles II's canal and avenue would be very important in determining the layout of Hampton Court when it was extensively rebuilt in the 1690s. That would take place after England had deposed its king for the second time in the seventeenth century. Charles's Catholic brother, James, Duke of York, had been the focus of bitter political fighting in an attempt to exclude him from the succession to the throne. Loyal London apprentices had even made their way out to Hampton Court in June 1681 to deliver a petition with 18,000 signatures supporting his right to succeed. The Duke's supporters won, and in 1685 he ascended the throne as James II. Within three years he had alienated most support and was to be driven from that throne in favour of a new Protestant king and queen, his son-in-law and daughter William III and Mary II, ruling as joint monarchs. Under them, the palace would be transformed.

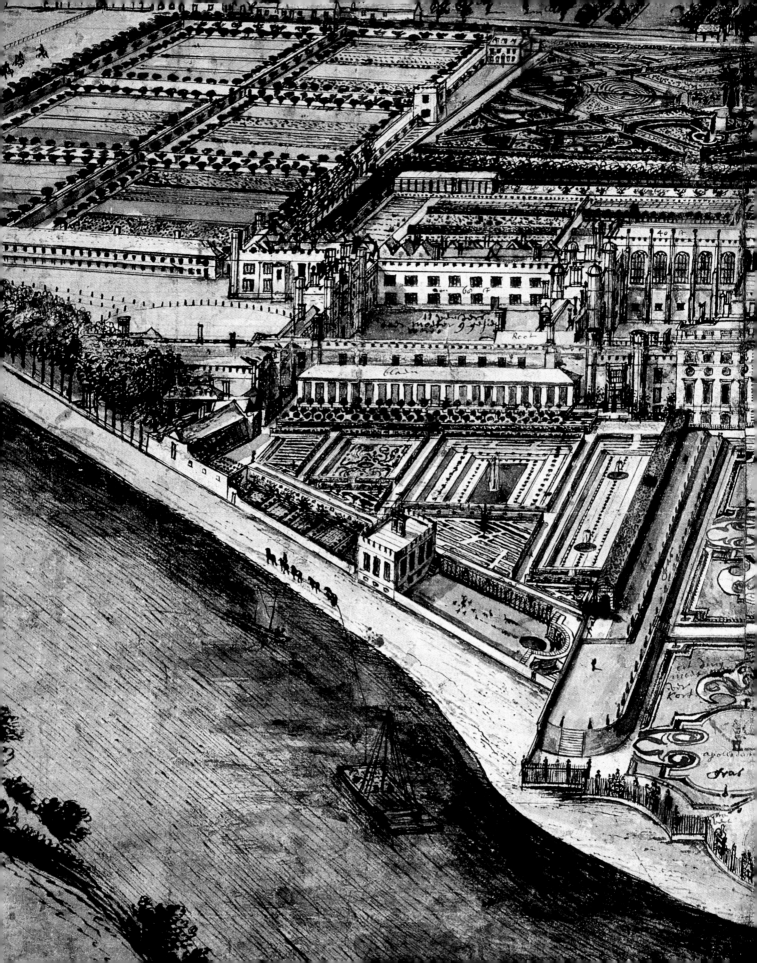

William and Mary's Hampton Court Palace 1689–1702

William of Orange (1689–1702; fig. 86) was a grandson of Charles I. In 1672 he had become the civil and military leader, or Stadtholder, of the Dutch Republic. His arranged marriage to his fifteen-year-old English cousin Mary (1689–94; fig. 87), also a grandchild of Charles I and the daughter of James, Duke of York (later James II), took place five years later. When Mary heard the news of her impending wedding, she 'wept all that afternoon and all the following day'. William took his new bride back to the Dutch Republic. There she had to learn the language as well as familiarize herself with the family's homes: the Renaissance-style Honselaarsdijk, the secluded 'House in the Wood' outside The Hague, and later Het Loo, the country house that William transformed into a private palace.

By 1688 James II doubted that his own daughter, although Protestant, would plot against him: 'you will be still as good a daughter to a father that has always loved you so tenderly', he told her. But William was making preparations to invade England. His fleet landed on 5 November 1688. On 13 February 1689, in the Banqueting House in Whitehall Palace, William and Mary were offered the Crown jointly in the presence of the assembled Lords and Commons, and promised to rule by law.

On 2 March the new King and Queen visited Hampton Court Palace. In the midst of such political turmoil, it is astonishing that they were able to devote so much time and effort to buildings. In July news of a Catholic plot to depose William actually interrupted celebrations for the birth of a son to his sister-in-law, the future Queen Anne, at Hampton Court. But the old Tudor palace, despite its being 'so very old built and so irregular', had many advantages as a home for this royal pair. Its clean air helped William's asthma. The monarchs' decision to relocate was not

85. (previous pages) Detail of a view of the palace from the south, c. 1702, by Leonard Knyff; see fig. 108.

86. The equestrian portrait of William III by Sir Godfrey Kneller, 1701, was probably commissioned by the King for the wall of the Presence Chamber on which it still hangs. The painting proclaimed the King's military skill and royal bearing.

87. Mary II by Sir Peter Lely, 1677. Mary loved her husband William, though she was frequently parted from him by his need to travel and campaign.

William and Mary's Hampton Court Palace, 1689–1702

88. Fountain Court, William and Mary's new quadrangle. The roundels on the facing wall contain panels painted by Louis Laguerre in 1691–94 with scenes from 'The Labours of Hercules'. William liked to associate himself with the classical hero Hercules, who performed superhuman feats.

universally popular; those involved in government found that 'the King's inaccessibleness and living so at Hampton Court altogether' made it difficult to get business done. So the royal couple also acquired the Earl of Nottingham's house in Kensington, then west of London, extending it to form the semi-metropolitan Kensington Palace.

Plans for rebuilding Hampton Court

No sooner had William and Mary visited Hampton Court than they began to plan improvements. By 4 May their architect, Sir Christopher Wren, presented them with an estimate of the building costs, meaning that the many different schemes documented in the designs produced by Wren's office had been judged, revised and finally accepted. Wren, Surveyor of the Royal Works, was a true polymath, a successful scientist before he turned to architecture. He had long wanted to build a royal palace, and found in Queen Mary a particularly sympathetic patron. Yet the project would also bring him trouble and humiliation.

The royal couple and Wren did not begin with a blank piece of paper. The Tudor palace already stood in a mature landscape, and Charles II's Long Water Canal was the obvious axis of the East Front of the new palace (fig. 68). Their initial thinking was radical: to demolish nearly all of the Tudor palace, retaining only Henry VIII's Great Hall at the centre of a grand Baroque entrance facing north (fig. 89). Double avenues marching south across Bushy Park would culminate in a vast semicircular courtyard built around the Great Hall. The green-fingered Earl of Portland, the Superintendent of the King's Gardens with the power 'to oversee and direct any plantations and works therein', began to plant the avenues, and they remain today.

It quickly became apparent that such a huge project would be difficult to finance and slow to build. Asthmatic William was anxious to move quickly. A greater part of the Tudor palace would have to be reused. In consequence, Nicholas Hawksmoor made one of the most important and useful drawings for architectural historians: a survey of the Tudor palace recording what William and Mary were about to destroy (fig. 90). Proposals were made to replace Henry VIII's lodgings and those of his queens with new south and east fronts around a new eastern quadrangle, Fountain Court (fig. 88). Both King and Queen, as joint monarchs, would have equally grand state apartments.

Hawksmoor drew up Wren's scheme based partly on a design by Claude Perrault for Louis XIV's palace of the Louvre in Paris, with

William and Mary's Hampton Court Palace, 1689–1702

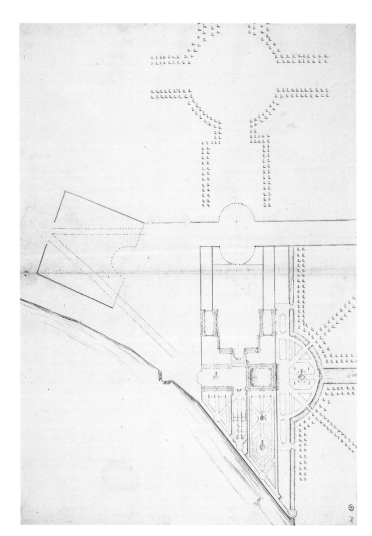

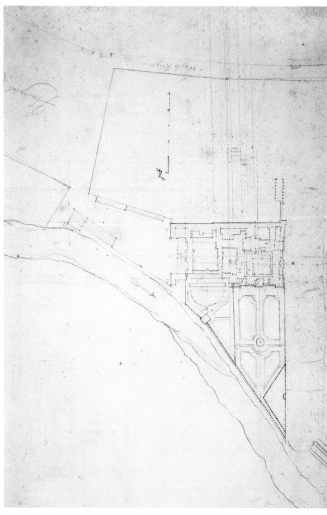

89. Nicholas Hawksmoor's site plan of the first projected scheme for rebuilding Hampton Court, 1689. The Great Hall remains in situ, while the palace is completely rebuilt around it in grand Baroque style.

90. Hawksmoor's record of the Tudor palace, 1689. This historically invaluable survey was made just before the south-eastern corner of the old palace of Henry VIII was demolished and rebuilt.

a giant pediment in the middle of the South Front and a dome at the centre of the east façade (fig. 91). The third, final set of elevations showed a more restrained, box-like palace. As built, Hampton Court's East Front features a row of round windows and is topped by a balustrade (fig. 92). The architectural writer Roger North was unimpressed, saying the balustrade 'looks like the teeth of a comb and doth in no sort answer the Grandeur of a Royall palace'. A carved triangular pediment marks the position of the main room on the principal (first) floor, and masks a low attic storey. Wren may have preferred to raise the *piano nobile* (containing the King's Apartments to the south and the Queen's to the east) slightly higher above the ground, but its level had to be carried through from the Great Hall and surviving first-floor lodgings of the Tudor palace.

Inside, the rooms were to be planned in a new manner. The gallery adjacent to William's rooms, the Cartoon Gallery, was unusually

The Story of Hampton Court Palace

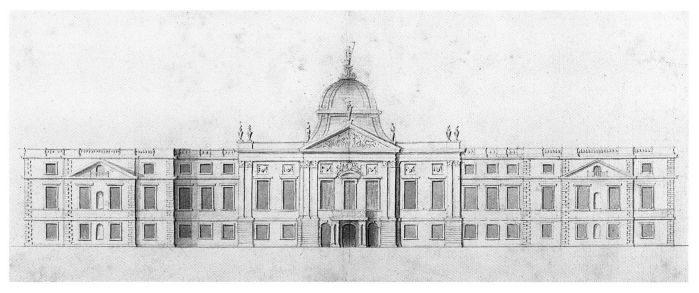

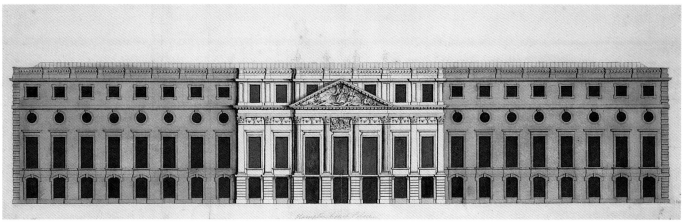

accessible for a royal long gallery: it opened directly into the Great Bedchamber, and from there to the Privy Chamber, the main room of parade in the middle of the South Front. The gallery was used for meetings of his council rather than as a private space for William himself. Like many features of the new Hampton Court, it was based directly on Versailles, the palace of William's arch-enemy Louis XIV, where a similar arrangement could be found.

Building work begins, 1689–94

It was Queen Mary who had the more detailed discussions with Wren, and the responsibility of driving the works forward. During the building season William would frequently be away campaigning on the continent against the French forces. One of the first tasks undertaken on site in 1689 was the construction of two blocks of barracks for William's

91. (top) Hawksmoor's proposed elevation of the East Front, 1689. This design for the Queen's Apartments was rejected.

92. Hawksmoor's eastern elevation of the palace as built, 1689. This was the final design for the East Front, shown in a finely worked presentation drawing. The scheme has elements in common with a proposed design for the palace of the Louvre by Bernini.

Foot and Horse Guards respectively (fig. 93), as protection for the vulnerable monarchs. The barracks flanking the drive leading to the West Front were begun in May and completed by the end of the year; in 1700 they were linked into one building by a 'sutlery' or provision room.

The building of the South Front of the new quadrangle began in June. The east range followed (fig. 94), and two years later the north range was begun. Hampton Court is well known for the glow of its red brick, but in fact Wren would have preferred to use more stone. His difficulty was that war against the French had made it dangerous for ships to carry stone up the Channel from Portland to London. Even work on Wren's new St Paul's Cathedral had ground to a halt for lack of supplies. Wren looked elsewhere: the carved swags on the South Front are made of Headington stone from Oxfordshire.

A builders' yard sprang up on the site of the Privy Garden to the south, including a rubbing house for decorative brickwork, a forge for ironwork and a 'closet' with a table for the architects' use. The bricks were bought from suppliers in Vauxhall and Twickenham; gravel was dug out of Hampton Court Green; Tudor stone from the old palace was reused; boards were brought from Charles II's unfinished palace at Winchester; and some of the joists in the Cartoon Gallery were simply Tudor timbers reshaped. Work forged ahead at a great pace until December, when disaster struck. A section of the spine wall collapsed and two carpenters died. Only weeks before, there had been a roof collapse at Wren's other project at Kensington Palace, and a workman had been killed there too. The Queen blamed herself: 'All this, as much as it was the fault of the workmen, humanly speaking,' she wrote, 'yet shewed me plainly the hand of God was in it, and I was truly humbled.'

On 13 January 1690, a hearing was held at the Treasury to determine the cause of the collapse, and to decide if the rest of the building was safe. On one side stood Wren. On the other stood Wren's architectural rival, the arrogant but successful William Talman. Wren needed to convince the Lords of the Treasury that he had indeed intended to use structural ironwork in the South Front; Talman argued that it was a desperate afterthought to fix a bad design. Wren triumphed and was

93. William III's Barrack Block was originally two buildings. The Horse Guards' accommodation lay nearer to Trophy Gate, while the Foot Guards lived closer to the palace. The guards remained until the early twentieth century.

The Story of Hampton Court Palace

allowed to resume work. A further section of brickwork was taken down and rebuilt for safety. Talman, however, would soon have his revenge.

Meanwhile, Mary was using the Water Gallery as a small private house while work was in progress on the main palace. This Tudor brick structure, originally used for disembarking from royal barges, had last been used by Charles II's retired mistress Lady Castlemaine, latterly Duchess of Cleveland (fig. 47). She had constructed a dairy within the gallery, an aristocratic playroom like that of Louis XIV's mistress Louise de La Vallière at Versailles. Daniel Defoe described how Mary now created within the gallery 'a set of lodgings, for her private retreat only, but most exquisitely furnished'. He thought it 'the pleasantest little Thing within Doors that could possibly be made'. The dairy had running hot and cold water, and was retiled in Delftware. On the first floor was a gallery, hung with the paintings of 'the principal ladies attending upon her majesty'. These were the portraits in Sir Godfrey Kneller's series of the 'Hampton Court Beauties' that now hang in William III's Private Dining Room (fig. 102).

The blue-and-white Delft tiles in the dairy provided the theme for the decoration throughout (fig. 96). Mary had become infected with the

94. The East Front today. The thirteen fountains of the Great Fountain Garden were originally intended to play before it. The yews in the foreground were planted in Queen Anne's time, but have grown immensely from their original tightly clipped shape.

William and Mary's Hampton Court Palace, 1689–1702

mania for interior decoration with blue-and-white china while in The Netherlands, and at Het Loo William and Mary had employed the designer Daniel Marot to oversee the design of such china-based rooms for them (fig. 95). His influence is seen throughout the Baroque palace here. Chairs for the Water Gallery were made in London, 'painted in imitation of china for our service at Hampton Court'. Despite the extravagance of the Water Gallery, it would soon be pulled down and a new Privy Garden constructed over its site.

Mary, one of the most significant among all Hampton Court's royal patrons, spent only six years supervising work there. In December 1694, while at Kensington Palace, she discovered a rash on her arms. Recognizing it as smallpox, she calmly set about ordering her affairs. 'If I should lose her, I shall have done with the world', William himself wrote, but on the 28th, Mary died. Despite its inauspicious beginning, theirs was a close marriage, and William was grief-stricken.

One consequence of Mary's death was that work stopped at Hampton Court. Her role as client had been vital, but a pause was necessary financially. The Queen and King had been spending at twice the rate of Charles II. They owed sixteen months' worth of salaries to their servants below stairs. A period of retrenchment was required.

95. (top) This blue-and-white japanned table, in the style of Daniel Marot, is by tradition associated with Hampton Court's Water Gallery. Remodelled for Mary II but demolished in the later phases of building the Baroque palace, the riverside building was the original setting for the Queen's famed blue-and-white collection.

96. One of the blue-and-white cream pans from Queen Mary's dairy in the Water Gallery. Delftware to designs by A. Kocx, c. 1694.

The completion of the King's State Apartments

In 1697 William's war against the French came to an end when the Peace of Rijswijk was signed. William found himself with time and money to spend at Hampton Court once again. He now had to solve the problem of how best to display the glorious series of cartoons, designs for tapestries, by Raphael depicting the *Acts of the Apostles*. Made in 1516 for tapestries intended for the Sistine Chapel, they had been acquired by Charles I (then Prince of Wales) in 1623. Now the cartoons were put up in the specially modified Cartoon Gallery (fig. 98), where Christopher Hatton reported them as 'far beyond all the paintings I ever saw'. (The cartoons on display now are copies, probably made by Henry Cooke in 1697, the originals having gone to the Victoria and Albert Museum in 1865.)

The Story of Hampton Court Palace

97. The Queen's Closet is hung with eight panels of embroidery, probably designed for Mary II by Daniel Marot. Although it was intended for her use, Mary died before this room could be completed.

This was but the first step in the process of finishing and furnishing the interiors (fig. 97). Wren's estimate for completion of the state apartments, at £6800, was undercut by that of William Talman, at £5500. Talman was duly commissioned to complete the Great Stair, Guard Chamber, Communication Gallery and 'four rooms beyond to the King's Great Bedchamber'. French taste was considered the height of fashion, then as always. These rooms owed a great debt to France. Charles II and James II had already introduced some of the habits and etiquette of the French court to England, and the trend continued.

98. The Cartoon Gallery was one of the first purpose-built picture galleries in Britain, built for William III to display Raphael's Acts of the Apostles. Today the room is hung with a set of seventeenth-century copies, which were painted in the gallery in 1697, probably by Henry Cooke.

99. Detail of a Grinling Gibbons architrave in the Cartoon Gallery. John Evelyn described the Dutch carver as 'the greatest master both for invention and rareness of work that the world ever had in any age'.

William and Mary's Hampton Court Palace, 1689–1702

100. (opposite) The decoration of the King's Staircase was not completed until after William III's death. Antonio Verrio, the high-living and sociable Italian artist who undertook the work, went on to decorate the Queen's Drawing Room for Queen Anne, but his deteriorating sight reduced the success of his later works.

A suite of royal rooms, formerly known as a 'lodging', gradually became known by the French term of an 'apartment'.

Talman had to base his designs for the King's Apartments around the Tudor tapestries that would still form the backbone of the rooms' decoration. Grinling Gibbons began work on carving in 1699; he provided architectural mouldings and carved festoons over many of the doors, as well as frames for the pictures over the mantelpieces and downstairs in the King's Private Apartments (fig. 99). The furnishing of these apartments was placed in the hands of Ralph, 1st Duke of Montagu, Master of the Great Wardrobe – an expert in fashion and style, having served as ambassador to France for five years. His London home, Montagu House, was itself a monument to French taste.

The rooms at Hampton Court were relatively sparsely furnished, mainly because space had to be left for the crush of courtiers when the King was in residence. The windows of the outer rooms are so tall that their curtains have to be pulled up by strings into festoons that disappear into a carved box covered in white damask. The more private rooms – the King's closets and gallery – had red and green curtains drawn sideways in the modern fashion. The decoration is

101. The King's Eating Room, with the portrait of the Danish king Christian IV and the tapestry of 'The Miraculous Draught of Fishes' from Raphael's Acts of the Apostles series. This bare interior would usually be set up only when the King dined in state.

The Story of Hampton Court Palace

William and Mary's Hampton Court Palace, 1689–1702

102. *The King's Private Dining Room, where Sir Godfrey Kneller's 'Hampton Court Beauties' are displayed. William III's dining table is set out with meringues and crystallized fruit for the third, or dessert, course of dinner.*

carefully graded and becomes increasingly elaborate in the more private rooms furthest away from the King's Staircase. The staircase itself (fig. 100) was painted by the Italian – and, controversially, Catholic – artist Antonio Verrio, who also painted the ceilings of the two innermost rooms of the King's Apartments, the Great and Little Bedchambers. On the staircase Verrio compared William III with Alexander the Great in triumphal mode, dominating a group of Roman emperors representing Catholic enemies, alongside a banquet of the gods denoting the peace and plenty that William had brought. A prominent figure here as elsewhere in the decoration of the new work was William's classical hero, Hercules, bearing his distinctive club and lion-skin.

In the Guard Chamber at the top of the stairs the weapons on the walls were arranged by John Harris, Furbisher of Small Arms, into a decoratively menacing scheme, although only the pikes, drums and armour survive from the seventeenth century. Most courtiers would pass through this room to reach the Presence Chamber and Privy Chamber with their canopied thrones, and from there, according to status, some could navigate deeper into the State Apartments.

The Story of Hampton Court Palace

As Hampton Court was completed for only a short period before
William died, it is difficult to picture his daily life. However, he does
seem to have appeared before his court more frequently at the evening
gathering known as the 'drawing room' rather than dining in public
in the Eating Room (fig. 101). He preferred to eat with his intimates,
just come in from the hunt, in his Private Dining Room on the ground
floor. Under the almond-shaped eyes of Kneller's 'Beauties', which were
moved here from the Water Gallery, William would frequently drink
too much in his depressed and lonely later years.

Since the time of Charles II, the bedchamber had become the
most important room in the palace for receiving visitors, rather than
a private room for the king alone. It is likely that William received
ambassadors in the Great Bedchamber, as Charles II had done before
him. This room demonstrates William's devotion to French fashion,
for his great red bed was probably a gift from Louis XIV to the diplomat
the Earl of Jersey, William's Lord Chamberlain, who then presented
it to the King (fig. 4). William brought out from storage a rail made for
Charles II, installing it around his bed in order to keep spectators back.
The Great Bedchamber was used for ceremony and the King would
sleep elsewhere. While he also had a Little Bedchamber next door

*103. The ceiling of the
King's Little Bedchamber
by Antonio Verrio, showing
Mars asleep in the lap
of Venus.*

William and Mary's Hampton Court Palace, 1689–1702

104. Design for the Great Fountain Garden by Daniel Marot, 1689. The thirteen fountains intended for this garden were constructed but never put into working order. Ornate iron gates by Jean Tijou separated the garden from the park. Beyond lie the two secondary avenues added by William and Mary to Charles II's central Long Water Avenue.

(fig. 103), he probably used his private apartments on the ground floor at night. The King's Back Stairway linked the State Apartments on the upper floor to his private apartments below. This also provided access to the adjacent rooms of the King's favourite, Arnold Joost van Keppel, Earl of Albemarle, who occupied a suite on the ground floor.

Grand opening

In 1699 the Lord Chamberlain's secretary Sir John Stanley was given the task of allocating the lodgings at Hampton Court to the members of William III's household. Sir Christopher Wren had made a survey of the building, and Stanley had merely to assign rooms to individuals. Rooms above the King's Apartments were reached by a narrow stair set within the thickness of the central spine of the building, so that their inhabitants would not disturb the royal occupants. Immediately below the Cartoon Gallery lay the small kitchens used among others by Mr Grice, the cook responsible for preparing William's newly fashionable drinking chocolate.

In the end no one was pleased, finding his or her rooms too high, too small, or not grand enough. Stanley's task was the final preparation

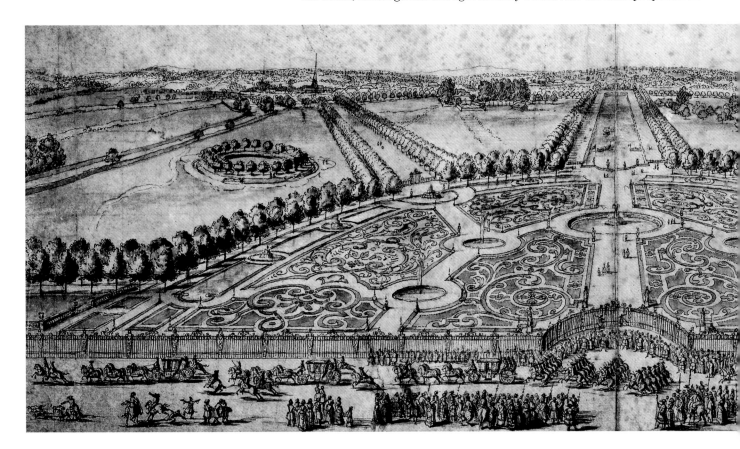

for a long-awaited occasion. The palace, transformed by the vision of
William III and Mary II, was at last ready to receive the first full visit
of the court. On 28 October, Robert Jennings reported that 'the King's
apartment is finished, and I fancy 'twill be made the prettiest place in
the world. The king will give us all country apartments; we shall be
much there, for he likes the place extremely.' Although the courtiers'
lodgings were still hurriedly being decorated, this was the end of
the lengthy process of designing and building. In the meantime,
William had lost his popularity, he was a sorrowing widower and the
opportunity for the devoted couple to enjoy their ambitious building
project together had never materialized.

As William had decided to use the Cartoon Gallery for meetings
of his council, he found himself without a private gallery for exercise
or informal conversation, so he commandeered the first-floor Queen's
Gallery, which had been planned for his wife on the East Front (fig. 135).
This room was decorated in green mohair, with back-chairs covered
in matching green. In 1702 the walls were hung with Mantegna's
Triumphs of Caesar, restored first by Parry Walton and secondly by
Louis Laguerre. The rest of the Queen's Apartments stood unfinished
and empty.

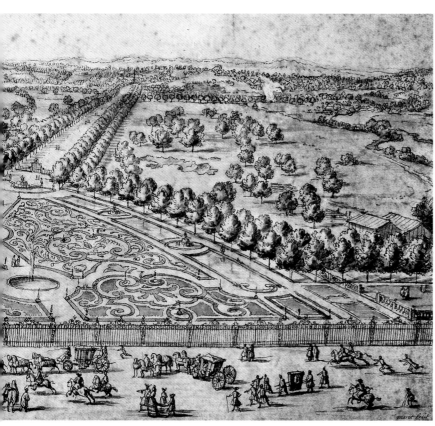

105. *During 1700 the
French smith Jean Tijou
provided 172 iron rails,
170 twisted pillars and
2752 square iron bars for
the Great Fountain Garden
at Hampton Court. The
detail illustrated here is
from his screen for the
Privy Garden.*

William and Mary's Hampton Court Palace, 1689–1702

106. Citrus aurantium
more *(the Seville orange)*
by Stephenus Cousijns.
This plant was one of the
exotics amassed by Mary II
and displayed at Hampton
Court. The Queen's
collection of exotics has
been restored in the past
ten years.

The transformation of the gardens

Meanwhile, as the courtiers settled into their new apartments, work was under way on the gardens outside. The Hampton Court gardens were the culmination of William's experience of creating gardens in The Netherlands. The details of the largest parterre ever created in the seventeenth century were under discussion even before the East Front of the palace was completed. The Great Fountain Garden was to contain thirteen fountains powered by the Longford River, occupying the semicircle of land between the palace and the park. Daniel Marot was paid just over £236 for its design in 1689 (fig. 104). Some areas were *parterre de broderie* (box hedges and gravel), while others were *gazon coupé* (grass and gravel intermingled in a complex design best appreciated from above).

On the South Front, garden works had to wait until the 1690s after the builders' yard had been cleared away. The King's Private Apartments on the ground-floor level incorporated an Orangery (the Upper Orangery) complete with stoves and orange trees, and its doors could be opened wide to allow the interior to flow into the exterior. The Tudor mount was removed in 1690, and it took ten years for the final form of William's Privy Garden to appear.

Henry Wise's garden design was marked by a major intervention on William's part. In June 1701, the Privy Garden was nearing completion, with its new fountain, terraces and boundary walls in place. The wrought-iron screens by Jean Tijou (fig. 105) were slung between poles to demonstrate the effect of their intended position between the garden and the river. William was dissatisfied because he could not see the water from his first-floor State Apartments – so he decided to lower the southern end of the garden by 90 centimetres (3 ft). This meant that all had to be removed and replaced. Five statues, *Bacchus, Ceres, Apollo and Marsyas, Vulcan* and *Apollo*, stood in the five garden compartments; further embellishments included sundials, lead urns, a central fountain, stone steps and, to the west, the long elmwood bower running along the top of a bank (fig. 108).

To the west of the Privy Garden lay the garden containing the Tudor ponds, now vastly improved with the construction of a Glass Case Garden and a new Banqueting House (fig. 107). The former contained three greenhouses built to Dutch designs for Mary's famous collection of exotic plants from around the world (fig. 106). William replaced them with the single surviving second Orangery (the Lower Orangery) after

107. *The Banqueting House, seen from the roof of the palace. The adjacent Pond Gardens contain Tudor walls and the remains of the Tudor fishponds that were made into gardens by Queen Mary II.*

108. *The Netherlandish artist Leonard Knyff is famous for his bird's-eye views of English country estates. Many were later engraved and published by John Kip. This view shows the palace from the south in c. 1702, when William III's Privy Garden had replaced that of Henry VIII and other monarchs.*

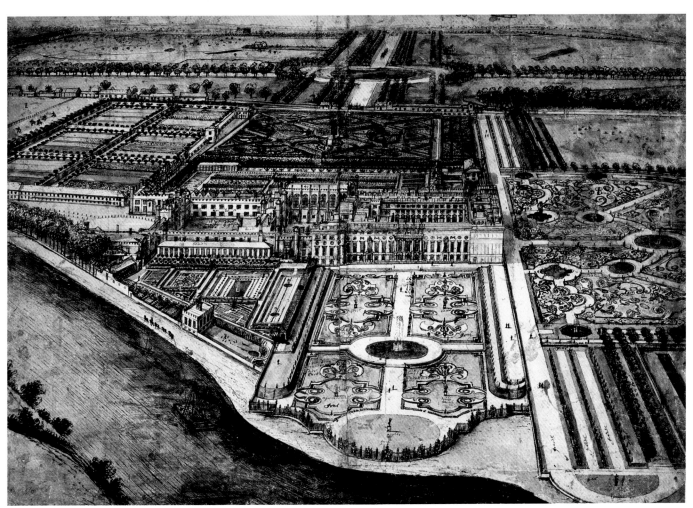

William and Mary's Hampton Court Palace, 1689–1702

109. The main room in
the Banqueting House
overlooks the river and
was intended for small-
scale entertainment. It is
decorated with murals by
Verrio and his assistants,
depicting, on the ceiling,
Minerva surrounded by
the arts and sciences and,
on the walls, the loves
of Jupiter.

her death. To the south, across the ponds, the Banqueting House has been described as Talman's most important and original surviving work at Hampton Court. The brick exterior, with its battlemented roof, is in harmony with the Tudor surroundings, but it contains a dramatic painted interior by Verrio and others, sumptuously up to date (fig. 109). The Banqueting House was the first stage of a plan to create a *ménagerie* like Louis XIV's at Versailles, though at Hampton Court work got only as far as the riverside aviary, containing oak birdcages and eighteen nesting boxes with bird-sized ramps leading up to them.

A further improvement to the gardens took place to the north, where William laid out the Wilderness Garden (fig. 110) in what had been the

109. The main room in the Banqueting House overlooks the river and was intended for small-scale entertainment. It is decorated with murals by Verrio and his assistants, depicting, on the ceiling, Minerva surrounded by the arts and sciences and, on the walls, the loves of Jupiter.

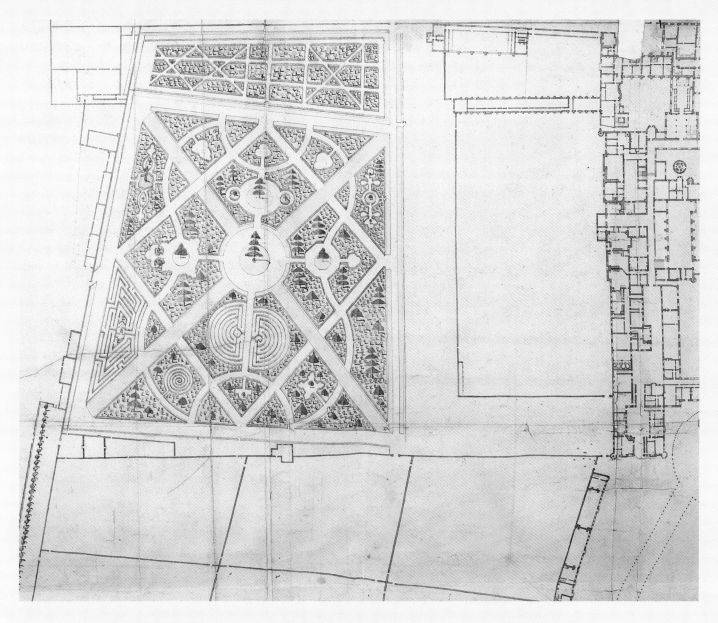

Tudor orchard. The Wilderness was a fairly formal style of garden by modern standards, a number of interconnected paths bordered by neatly clipped high hedges of hornbeam, creating a geometrical network of pathways in which the wanderer could pleasurably lose his or her way. One of the compartments of the Wilderness took this concept to its extreme: it was laid out with the tight twists and turns of Hampton Court's famous Maze (fig. 111). Because the documentary evidence is sparse, historians continue to debate exactly when the Hampton Court Maze was planted. William III's courtiers probably found the paths between its hedges as amusing and enticing as visitors do today. In 1724 Daniel Defoe would describe the 'labyrinth' as 'not only well designed, and completely finished, but ... perfectly well kept'.

110. The earliest representation of the Maze at Hampton Court is on this anonymous plan of the palace and gardens, executed in the Office of Works, c. 1714. The surviving Maze is in the bottom left compartment of the (northern) Wilderness Garden. Other spirals and labyrinths shown no longer survive.

William and Mary's Hampton Court Palace, 1689–1702

111. *The Maze is the only surviving compartment of the once extensive Wilderness north of the palace, originally planted in deciduous hornbeam. The tough yew of the hedges today is a twentieth-century replanting; the original hedges were damaged by the huge number of visitors in the nineteenth and twentieth centuries.*

The Story of Hampton Court Palace

Originally the Wilderness contained four mazes, all but one of which are now lost. Still this is not the end of the list of pleasant places made for William III. A short walk away along the river to the east, he had the Bowling Green and its four pavilions reconstructed to Talman's designs (fig. 112). Each pavilion, similar to those at Louis XIV's country palace at Marly, contained three rooms on its upper floor. One pavilion survives, much altered, as a private house in the park.

The King's death

Then, on 20 February 1702, when riding his horse Sorrel out from Hampton Court, William fell after the animal stumbled. He had his broken collarbone set, then misguidedly travelled to Kensington Palace. There, after a few days of deteriorating health, he died. Jacobites, supporters of the claims of the Catholic sons of the deposed James II against the Protestant King William, drank toasts to a certain 'little gentleman in black velvet', the Hampton Court mole whose hill had caused the horse to trip. But the new palace was built and the Protestant kingdom was secure, twin legacies of William and Mary.

112. J. Tinney after Anthony Highmore, The Pavilions belonging to the Bowling Green, at the End of the Terras Walk, at Hampton Court, c. 1744. *The four pavilions around the oval-shaped bowling green were designed by William Talman as retiring places for William III and his courtiers between games.*

William and Mary's Hampton Court Palace, 1689–1702

Two Queens and Two Georges 1702–60

Queen Anne (1702–14)

When Queen Anne (fig. 114) came to the throne in 1702 in succession to her brother-in-law, William III, the era of grand spending on Hampton Court Palace came to a swift close. Significant work continued, within the palace and in the gardens and estate, but the main shape that survives to this day had already been laid down.

Anne was constantly beset by money worries. She was reluctant to settle William's outstanding debts on the palace, and many craftsmen went unpaid. The grant made by Parliament was insufficient for her needs. The Office of Works was, if anything, in even worse financial straits. Anne was committed to expensive military ventures, at least until the Duke of Marlborough's magnificent victory over Louis XIV's France at Blenheim in 1704. The Queen also had constant health worries. In her younger years she was almost continually pregnant, but of seventeen pregnancies only one son survived even into childhood. In later years, especially after she was widowed, she grew obese and suffered from gout and a host of other ailments.

Added to these difficulties was the politically and socially inconvenient fact that the reigning monarch was a woman. Although Anne occupied the apartments designed for the king's use at each of her palaces, the political advantage of ready access to a male monarch by male courtiers was now lost. Even Queen Anne's close companion, Sarah, Duchess of Marlborough, the wife of the Blenheim victor and Groom of the Stole, said the Queen retained in her prodigious memory 'very little besides ceremonies and customs of courts and suchlike insignificant trifles'. The reign of Queen Anne was a watershed, ushering in an age of party politics and cabinet government in which the monarch became more of a ceremonial figure, less a focus of political activity and patronage.

The Queen preferred Windsor as a country retreat, just as in London her preference was for Kensington Palace rather than the

113. (previous pages) Anthony Highmore, The Diagonal Walk, Fountain and Canal in the Garden of Hampton Court, 1744; see fig. 132.

114. Queen Anne by Sir Godfrey Kneller, c. 1702–04. By the end of her life the Queen became so obese and diseased that she was barely able to walk. A short poem in praise of Anne at Hampton Court, written in 1704, proclaimed, 'Here our blest Queen's magnificence yet reigns'.

sovereign's official seat, St James's Palace. Hampton Court was mainly a place for business, being midway between central London and Windsor and so quite convenient for politicians to assemble there for Privy Council meetings. In the first six years of her reign, Anne spent only three nights in the palace. Her beloved husband, Prince George of Denmark – 'very fat, loves news, his bottle and the Queen', as one contemporary described him – died in 1708. After this Anne made greater use of Hampton Court, and in the last four years of her life she devoted her efforts to improving and embellishing it.

When William III died, the principal building works at Hampton Court were complete. The East Front contained the shell of the range intended as the Queen's Apartments, unfinished since Mary II's death in 1694. The intertwined monogram of William and Mary poignantly forms one of the pre-eminent decorative motifs on the exterior of the range. Once Antonio Verrio had completed the magnificent painted decoration on the King's Staircase, he was given the task of providing the decorative scheme for the Queen's Drawing Room. The principal

115. Antonio Verrio's mural on the south wall of the Queen's Drawing Room showed Prince George of Denmark (top left), consort to Queen Anne, in a pose rare in the history of royal portraiture: naked and riding a sea creature. Prince George inhabited the Queen's Apartments as Anne, being monarch, was occupying the King's.

Two Queens and Two Georges, 1702–60

room in the East Front, centred on the Long Water Canal and the formal gardens, this room was almost certainly fitted out for Prince George. He features twice in its decoration: on the north wall he stands dressed as Lord High Admiral, reviewing the fleet; on the opposite wall a figure traditionally supposed to be his, naked and plump, lies on the back of a sea creature with cherubs disporting themselves around him (fig. 115). The rest of the decorative scheme glorifies Anne and British naval power. Around this magnificence, other rooms remained unfinished; some even still lacked floorboards.

In 1707 the Astronomical Clock and the cupola above Anne Boleyn's Gateway were both overhauled, and a new mechanism was provided for the clock. These were among the few exterior works undertaken at Hampton Court in the first half of Anne's reign. She resided there for a total of five months in 1710, 1711 and 1713, and various alterations were made to the King's Apartments, reflecting both the Queen's position as a female monarch, for whom the ceremonial *levée* was somewhat inappropriate, and her general ill-health. The back stairs were used much more frequently as a means of access by courtiers, ambassadors and petitioners.

When the court was in residence the palace was full and busy once more, a centre of political intrigue and decision-making. Alexander Pope described in his poem *The Rape of the Lock* (1712) the assemblies, jockeying for preferment and social ritual of the reinvigorated Hampton Court Palace:

> *Here Thou, Great Anna!*
> *Whom three Realms obey,*
> *Dost sometimes Counsel take –*
> *and sometimes Tea.*

The greatest impact that Queen Anne had upon the fabric of the palace was remodelling the Chapel Royal (fig. 117). A firm upholder of the Anglican faith and royal tradition, she maintained a full complement of chapel musicians. As a sick woman who did not care

116. Ceiling of the remodelled Royal Pew by Sir James Thornhill, 1711. Thornhill was employed by both Queen Anne and George I at Hampton Court, and spent his later years copying the Raphael cartoons in the palace.

The Story of Hampton Court Palace

for the elaborate etiquette of the Bedchamber, she saw her daily
attendance at Chapel as her main opportunity to make a public
appearance. In 1710 Wren and Hawksmoor successfully presented
schemes for remodelling the body of the Chapel; these included a
grand timber reredos at the east end, the removal of the Tudor window
tracery and the addition of panelling, box pews, an organ and new
sanctuary fittings. A staircase was added leading down from the Royal

117. *Sir Christopher Wren
radically changed the
Chapel Royal for
Queen Anne. The Tudor
windows were replaced with
large casements (replaced in
their turn with copies of the
original windows in 1894).
A* trompe l'œil *window
painted by Thornhill on the
south wall next to the organ
preserves the appearance of
Wren's windows.*

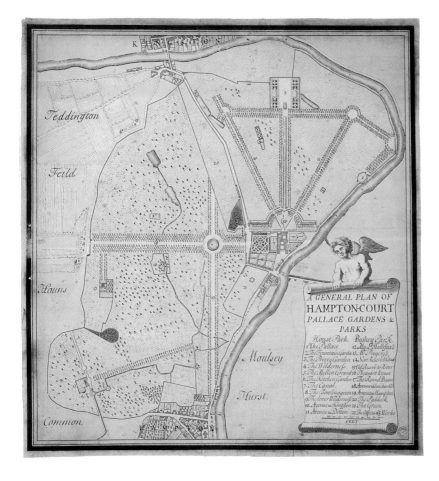

Pew, where James Thornhill painted the central ceiling with a playful scene of cherubs in the heavens holding aloft a crown and a sword (fig. 116).

When she was at Hampton Court but not in her bed or her pew, the Queen could be found in the park indulging her love of hunting. Unable to ride on horseback, she followed the hunt in a two-wheeled chaise for which 32 kilometres (20 miles) of new rides were cut through Home Park and Bushy Park. She was certainly vigorous, as Jonathan Swift recorded that 'The queen was hunting the stag till four this afternoon, and she drove in her chaise above forty miles, and it was five before we went to dinner.'

In contrast to the limited work inside the palace, the gardens were well maintained. There was a complete remodelling of the Great Parterre and the Great Fountain Garden. Henry Wise, who became the royal gardener in 1702, supervised the scheme (fig. 118). He simplified the layout, removed the box hedging (the smell of which, according to Daniel Defoe, Queen Anne detested) and the cut

118. (above) Charles Bridgeman, A General Plan of Hampton Court Palace Gardens and Parks, 1711. This important survey of the Hampton Court estate at the end of Queen Anne's reign records the alterations made to the gardens by Henry Wise, whom Bridgeman succeeded as Master Gardener in 1728.

119. The Great Fountain Garden looking east. Queen Anne was keen to reduce expenditure on the royal gardens, and the Great Fountain Garden was much simplified during her reign.

The Story of Hampton Court Palace

turf patterns, but kept the yew trees. The result was a simpler garden design in grass and gravel that was more English than French in taste (fig. 119). The ironwork screen by Jean Tijou was finally put in its intended place at the river end of the Privy Garden. The Lion Gate, a grand new north entrance to the gardens from Bushy Park, was planned, although not completed until the following reign. With its military motifs this was almost certainly the work of Sir John Vanbrugh, playwright and gentleman-architect, who came to greater prominence at the palace after the Queen's death. On a visit in 1703, he and his companion 'were sopping our arses in the Fountain, for you must know we have got some warm weather at last'.

George I and the Hanoverian Dynasty (1714–27)

Queen Anne died in August 1714. The following month her successor arrived to claim his new kingdom: George, Elector of Hanover (fig. 120). A stout Protestant (in both senses), George I was the great-grandson of James I through the female line. The new King brought German courtiers and Turkish servants, his mistresses (he had divorced his wife in 1694 and locked her away), and his son, the future George II, with his wife, Caroline of Ansbach (figs. 121 and 122), and their young family. The new King also supported the Whigs politically, in contrast to the favour the old queen had bestowed on their Tory rivals. Many Tories were implicated in the 1715 Jacobite rebellion, which intended to return the exiled Stuart line in the shape of Queen Anne's Catholic half-brother James to the throne. With the abject failure of the rising, Tories were to be consigned to the political wilderness for a generation.

George I also smiled upon Hampton Court Palace, where Vanbrugh was his preferred designer, assisted at first by Nicholas Hawksmoor. Sir Christopher Wren, who had dominated the royal building programme and the Office of Works for so long, was ousted in 1718 and a new generation of architects took control. The main work at the palace was to fit out suitably impressive suites of rooms for the Prince and Princess of Wales on the queen's side of the palace: the Bedchamber (fig. 124), Drawing Room and Privy Chamber. Lord Hervey, whose journals provide vivid descriptions of court

120. George I in his coronation robes by Bernard Lens, 1718. The King's accession was swiftly followed by the attempt of the 'Old Pretender', James Edward Stuart, heir to James II, to regain the throne; that failed, and the strength of the Hanoverian dynasty was confirmed.

life in the subsequent reign, wrote 'the pageantry and splendour, the badges and trappings of royalty, were as pleasing to the son as they were irksome to the father'.

An abiding theme of the Hanoverian era was the mutual loathing between royal fathers and their eldest sons. The often-bitter enmity between George I and George II, George II and Prince Frederick, Prince Frederick and George III, and finally George III and George IV was in itself the focus of political intrigue. In George I's reign Hampton Court became the country version of Leicester House, the London home of the Prince of Wales, which attracted both a political opposition and an alternative

121. Sir James Thornhill's portrait of George, Prince of Wales, in the coving of the Queen's State Bedchamber. The Board of Works considered the ceiling 'skilfully and laboriously performed'.

122. Thornhill's matching portrait of Caroline, Princess of Wales, in the coving of the Queen's State Bedchamber. King George I and Frederick, later Prince of Wales, are also portrayed on the ceiling.

123. Queen Caroline's Bathroom, fitted out for her as Princess of Wales. The room and furnishings were restored in 1995. The Queen would sit on a stool inside the tub while she bathed. The marble cistern provided cold water; the Queen's Necessary Woman brought in hot water from the back stairs.

artistic group. In 1716 when George I returned to Hanover, leaving the Prince of Wales in charge (but stopping short of making him Regent), the Prince led a glittering court and conducted political business at Hampton Court Palace throughout those summer months.

Of the rooms that were newly fitted out for the Prince and Princess in 1716, the most significant was the Queen's State Bedchamber, sumptuously furnished with a new state bed under a ceiling by Thornhill, the walls hung with Stuart royal portraits. The decorative scheme proclaimed the rightful descent of the Crown to the Hanoverian princes. In addition to the State Rooms, the royal couple were provided with a number of private rooms in the north-east corner of the State Apartments, including a bathroom (fig. 123) and dressing-room each. Their private bedroom still retains the night lock system by which the Prince or Princess could lie in bed and control the doors by a system of wires and bolts.

In 1716, and then again in 1717 when the King resided at Hampton Court together with his son and daughter-in-law, these rooms must have been swarming with builders and decorators as soon and as often as there was opportunity. The works programme was extended in 1717 to include the decoration by Vanbrugh of the Guard Chamber (fig. 125)

124. The Queen's State Bedchamber, incomplete after the death of Mary II and finished for the Prince and Princess of Wales only in 1716. The room still retains its original crimson silk damask bed, made for the royal couple in 1715.

125. Banqueting Hall
(the Queen's Guard
Chamber) by R. Reeve
after R. Cattermole, from
W.H. Pyne's History of
the Royal Residences
(1819). When first
completed, the room was
painted white and glazed
to give the effect of stone.
It was furnished with beds
and benches for the Yeomen
of the Guard.

126. Detail of the fireplace
in the Queen's Guard
Chamber, combining the
wit of Sir John Vanbrugh
and the skill of Grinling
Gibbons.

127. The fireplace in the
Queen's Presence Chamber,
designed by Sir John
Vanbrugh and probably
executed by Grinling
Gibbons.

and Presence Chamber, the two rooms that completed the formal circuit of the State Apartments, fulfilling the vision of William and Mary. The scheme included the over-sized figures of Yeomen of the Guard that flank the Guard Chamber fireplace (fig. 126), which have been attributed to Grinling Gibbons, and the chunky, idiosyncratic fireplaces in other rooms (fig. 127). The Prince's suite even acquired a new kitchen – the austere block to the north of the palace, known today as the Georgian House – which some now claim to be by Colen Campbell and the first Neo-Palladian English building (fig. 128).

The summer of 1717 at Hampton Court proved not to be the reconciliation between father and son that many had hoped for, but instead the opening skirmishes of a family war that lasted ten years. After 1717 the Queen's Private Apartments were

128. *John Spyers*, The East View of the North Inferior Court, *c. 1780. The Georgian House (left) was built as a separate kitchen block in 1717 for George I to designs possibly by Colen Campbell. It was known as the 'German' kitchen, as it was staffed by the cooks and servants brought to England by the King in 1715.*

129. *Thomas Fort's survey of the Great Hall set up as a theatre, c. 1718. Only with the antiquarian revival almost a century later was Henry VIII's hall uncovered once more. The stage may be seen at the top; the canvas scenery was painted by Thornhill.*

used no more (until George and Caroline themselves became King and Queen in 1727), as the Prince of Wales set up his own rival summer court at Richmond Lodge. The King was determined to make an even bigger splash at Hampton Court. In 1718 the Tudor Tennis Court was refurbished and converted for use as a grand assembly room, while the Great Hall was converted into a theatre (fulfilling the intentions of William III, who had begun to fit it out for the purpose; fig. 129). This work was probably by Vanbrugh, himself a playwright and theatre impresario. Curtains covered the windows, boxes and seats were installed, and the assembled audience faced west towards the stage in front of the screens passage. Sir Richard Steele's company from Drury Lane performed seven plays before the assembled court, including, appropriately, Shakespeare's *Hamlet* and *Henry VIII*.

The court of George I was relatively informal compared with that of preceding kings. The polished etiquette of the Bedchamber and the *levée* hardly outlived William III. The King occupied the full set of rooms built for William. He dined formally but usually not in state, so lesser mortals could join him at his table. He also instituted a more rigid separation between his private and his public apartments. The Gentlemen of the Bedchamber organized admission to the royal presence, guiding visitors up the back stairs to a closet accessible from the King's bedroom, where they were received.

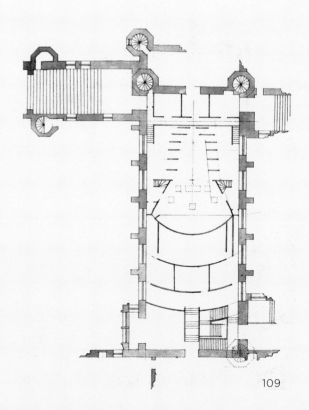

In the years following the visit of 1718, ambitious plans for the wholesale remodelling of Hampton Court were drawn up by Vanbrugh, but came to nothing. The Queen's Apartments were completed with the addition of an octagonal private oratory. Its rich and distinctive late-seventeenth-century domed carved timber ceiling had been kept in store for some thirty years and was installed in 1719. The King paid occasional visits to the palace, usually to hunt, but otherwise it sat shut up and idle, waiting for its next blaze of glory under the new monarch.

George II and Queen Caroline (1727–60)

When George II succeeded his father in 1727, Hampton Court Palace entered its final phase as a principal royal residence. King George and Queen Caroline were more frequent visitors than their immediate predecessors, especially the Queen, who regularly spent summers at Hampton Court when the King was away in Hanover. The work begun ten years before on the private rooms in the Queen's Apartments was completed, and soon new works were to be undertaken to accommodate the younger members of the large royal family.

These seasons at the royal court are colourfully documented in the memoirs and letters of Lord Hervey, made Vice-Chamberlain by Sir Robert Walpole, the prime minister, in April 1730. Hervey became the particular confidant of Queen Caroline. His main duty was the daily organization and upkeep of the royal palaces, assigning courtiers' lodgings, supervising the arrangements for moving the court physically from one palace to another, and planning special events. With his own lodgings at the foot of the Queen's back stairs, Hervey was in a strategic position to control private access to the royal presence and to know courtiers' movements.

Soon after he arrived at court, Hervey wrote to his lover Stephen Fox:

We jog on here le vieux train [in our usual way]. A little walking, a little hunting and a little playing; a little flattering, a little railing and a little lying; a little hate, a little friendship, and a little love; a little hope and a little fear, a little joy and a little pain.

Days usually started slowly. Every afternoon, before or after the 3 pm dinner (depending on the season), ladies walked in the gardens or parks (fig. 132), gossiping and flirting with their admirers. Tea was one of the lubricants of fashionable daytime activity. The evenings were often given to board or card games and dancing. 'No mill-horse ever went in a more constant track, or more unchanging circle', as Hervey put it.

Life at Hampton Court, a summer residence, was less formal in its routine than the winter season at St James's Palace. When they dined in public (which George I had disdained), the King and Queen usually had a crowd of onlookers. Their table at Hampton Court was described in 1733 as 'surrounded by benches to the very ceiling, which are filled with an infinite number of spectators'. There were days for the conduct of formal business, including the King's morning *levée* when he received ministers, ambassadors and other guests, and a formal 'drawing room' in the later evening in which the royal family circulated before retiring to the private apartments, where closer friends could attend on them.

With the court in residence the palace was full to bursting. All the members of the royal family had their own bodies of servants. Every officer of the royal household had the right to occupy an apartment. Others found accommodation where they could, within the palace or close at hand. Significant

131. (above) Mistress to George II, Henrietta Howard, Countess of Suffolk, lived in rooms above the Queen's Apartments to be near by when the King came to call. She retired to her Thames-side villa at Marble Hill in 1733.

132. Anthony Highmore, The Diagonal Walk, Fountain and Canal in the Garden of Hampton Court, 1744. Highmore was one of many artists whose work helped to make the Hampton Court gardens some of the most famous and influential in Europe.

Two Queens and Two Georges, 1702–60

133. Philippe Mercier, The Music Party: Frederick, Prince of Wales with his Three Eldest Sisters, *painted in c. 1733 when Prince Frederick began playing the cello. There is another version of this picture with the sitters in front of the Dutch House, now known as Kew Palace.*

improvements were made in 1731, with new furnishings for all the courtiers' lodgings. For the many hundreds who attended at court, it was – as it had been for centuries – an expensive place to be, but it held out the hope of preferment to office or an advantageous marriage. Alexander Pope satirized the dissembling, spite-driven gossip and flirtation, and the fawning on the most powerful courtiers for the advantages they could confer. Such arch criticism rankled. In his anonymous 'Epistle to a Doctor of Divinity from a Nobleman at Hampton Court', written in 1733, Lord Hervey directed his satire back against Pope:

... Like you, we lounge & feast & play & chatter
In private satirize, in public flatter.

By the time these lines were written, political opposition revolved around the figure of Prince Frederick and his court. Relations between father and son continued at a low ebb, and Hervey noted: 'Whenever the Prince was in a room with the King, it put one in mind of stories one has heard of ghosts that appear to be part of the company and are invisible to the rest.' The Prince's own mother, Queen Caroline, said she could not stand the sight of the 'avaricious, sordid monster' who was 'the greatest beast in the whole world'.

Despite the growing animosity between father and son, some of the most distinctive contributions to the ensemble at Hampton Court Palace were the newly refurbished rooms for the Prince of Wales in the north-east corner of the State Apartments. These were elaborately redecorated and refurnished in green and silver from 1728. Throughout the palace there was a programme of modernization that continued for the ten years following George II's accession, creating a suitable setting for the court on its regular summer forays. In 1731 the King refurbished the State Apartments and extended his private apartments. For most of this work the sumptuous new furnishings and fittings were designed by William Kent (who had been commissioned by George I for the decorative schemes in the State Apartments at Kensington Palace), and supplied by Benjamin Goodison. Meanwhile, the recently acquired (and shockingly French) Alexander tapestries celebrating Alexander the Great were hung in the Queen's Gallery (fig. 135), again with new furnishings by Kent. Verrio's murals in the Queen's Drawing Room, which Queen Caroline detested, were covered with green damask, and Mantegna's nine great paintings of the *Triumphs of Caesar* were hung on top.

The need for better accommodation, and the dilapidated state of the redundant Tudor royal apartments in Clock Court (fig. 134), provided

The Story of Hampton Court Palace

William Kent in 1732 with one of his most idiosyncratic palace commissions. For William, Duke of Cumberland, the King and Queen's second and favoured son, little expense was spared in providing a suitable set of apartments. Kent designed the new range in a self-consciously Gothic style, wrapped around the Tudor core that in part remains at the heart of the new building (fig. 136). The Tudor, Gothic and Jacobean elements in Kent's design (fig. 137), both inside and outside the range, were not archaeologically correct, and there were fantasy cupolas and turrets on the skyline that were removed in the 1850s, but this was nevertheless a deliberate attempt to make a fitting complement to the original sixteenth-century fabric. Sir Robert Walpole was said to have insisted that this building be Gothic, while the terracotta roundels taken from Whitehall's Holbein Gate were added to complete the Tudor effect.

The final embellishment of the palace under George II was the completion of the Queen's Staircase in 1734–35, again by William Kent. This had remained a plain space since the time of Mary II, in complete contrast to the King's Staircase. Pride of place was given to Gerrit van Honthorst's vast canvas *Mercury Presenting the Liberal Arts to Apollo and Diana* (fig. 72), representing Charles I and Henrietta Maria, and originally commissioned for the Banqueting House at Whitehall. Kent painted the walls with a series of *trompe l'œil* niches and half-domed spaces with classical sculptures in them, and the Garter star and royal ciphers within the ceiling scheme. His design for a complementary Garter star state bed seems, sadly, not to have been realized.

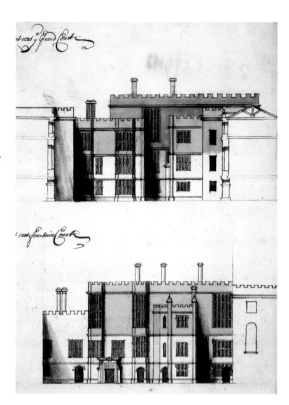

134. *The east elevation of Clock Court, 1727, attributed to Thomas Fort. This is a rare detailed view, prior to their replacement by William Kent in 1732, of the decayed royal lodgings built by Cardinal Wolsey for Henry VIII, Katherine of Aragon and Princess Mary.*

135. *The Queen's Gallery later became known as the Tapestry Gallery after the Alexander tapestries that George II installed there. The marble chimneypiece by John Nost was originally installed in the King's Great Bedchamber but was taken down almost immediately and moved here in 1701.*

In George I's reign the gardens had remained little altered from Queen Anne's time. Henry Wise, who had also been her Royal Gardener, generally maintained the status quo. His only significant change was to move the Tijou screen from the end of the Privy Garden to beside the park. In 1728 Charles Bridgeman succeeded Wise. He followed Queen Caroline's wishes in reducing formality and increasing the naturalistic effects in the gardens. In the Privy Garden, for example, the elaborate beds were grassed over, although the gardeners continued to keep the topiary in trim. It was in these gardens – celebrated in prints and engravings – that courtiers walked, gossiped and flirted (fig. 138). Bridgeman's tenure lasted ten years. George Lowe and then John Greening succeeded him. Real change came only after 1764, in the next reign, when Lancelot Brown was appointed.

The problem of inter-generational rivalry continued, meanwhile. The Queen believed her son to be impotent, and when – after some false starts – the Prince of Wales married 'the most decent and prudent' Augusta of Saxe-Gotha in 1736, the Queen doubted the reality of her daughter-in-law's first pregnancy. She told Walpole, 'Sir Robert, we shall be catched. At her labour I positively will be [present] ... I will be sure it is her child.' Her son chose to disregard this, and the denouement of this family saga was played out at Hampton Court Palace. On 31 July 1737, the Prince and Princess of Wales dined in state there with the King and Queen, but after dinner the Princess went into labour. As soon as the contractions started, the Prince rushed his wife away on a painful 24-kilometre (15-mile) carriage journey to St James's Palace. Since it was shut up for the summer, the baby was born on a bed covered with tablecloths, 'a little rat of a girl, about the bigness of a good large toothpick case'.

The Story of Hampton Court Palace

The other members of the royal family were unaware of this drama and played cards until bedtime. Roused at one in the morning, the Queen and her party sped from Hampton Court and arrived at St James's before dawn.

Shunned now by his parents, the Prince's rival court became a new focus of loyalty. 'Popularity always makes me sick,' the Queen said, 'but Fritz's popularity makes me vomit.' When the royal family and their attendants left Hampton Court at the end of October 1737 to return to St James's Palace, it was for the last time. The Queen was seriously ill with complications stemming from her own last pregnancy, and she died on 20 November.

King George II lived for another twenty-three years, but he never took the court back to Hampton Court in the summer again. He visited occasionally, especially when he called on his prized stables and horse stud in Home Park. He would undress and get into bed to rest, and Secretary of State William Pitt would kneel on a cushion at the bedside to conduct business with him.

Meanwhile, the palace's accessibility increased with the building in 1753 of the first bridge across the Thames. It began to attract visitors, who paid the housekeeper a small sum to allow them to enjoy the architectural and artistic splendours. The very first guidebook to Hampton Court Palace was published in 1742, as the second volume of George Bickham's *Deliciae Britannicae*. The circuit Bickham prescribed remained the visitor route around the palace for the next 250 years, a period in which Hampton Court ceased to be an occupied royal residence and became a place for public enjoyment and private accommodation.

136. *(opposite, top) George II's Gateway, Clock Court. William Kent replaced the Tudor royal range with an early essay in Georgian gothic; the four Maiano roundels were reset in the gateway. The principal rooms provided accommodation for the King's second son, the Duke of Cumberland.*

137. *(opposite, bottom) The ornate Jacobean ceiling in the suite for the Duke of Cumberland complemented William Kent's Tudor Gothic experiment on the exterior of the building.*

138. *Anthony Highmore,* A Perspective View of the East Front of Hampton Court taken from the Park Gate, *1744, showing clipped conical yews and the gardens peopled with visitors.*

The 'Grace-and-Favour' Palace after 1760

The second half of the palace's history, from 1760 to the present day, is one of increasing openness, first to new types of residents and then to the visiting public, coupled with a growing recognition of its important place in the history of English architecture. With the early death of Frederick, Prince of Wales, in 1751 the succession passed to his son George, who became George III in 1760 at his grandfather's death. The new King received the news at Kew – which had its own place in the history of royal building and residence in the next forty years – and Hampton Court was now effectively abandoned as a royal dwelling. There is a tradition that George II lost his temper at Hampton Court with his grandson, striking Prince George and instilling in him the lasting dislike he felt for the palace. The story is barely plausible, since the two are unlikely to have been there at the same time, but whatever the reason, both Hampton Court Palace and Kensington Palace seemed tainted by their associations with past family unhappiness, and George III (1760–1820) chose not to live in either of them.

George bought Buckingham House (called the Queen's House and later Buckingham Palace) as a domestic alternative to the formality and antiquated arrangements of St James's Palace, the sovereign's official London residence. Among the many treasures raided from Hampton Court Palace and brought to the Queen's House were the Raphael cartoons. When fire broke out in outbuildings at Hampton Court in 1770, the King said that he would not have been sorry if the whole place had burned down. His attention turned instead to Windsor Castle, little regarded by the royal family for the previous sixty years, and it became once again the principal royal retreat outside London. In the last years before his death in 1820 Windsor was the place of incarceration for the senile, 'mad' King (his unpredictable behaviour has been diagnosed as the inherited metabolic condition of porphyria, or as bipolar disorder).

Although his visits to Hampton Court were rare, George III interested himself considerably in the palace's affairs and ensured that the building was properly maintained. Verrio's mural paintings on the King's Staircase were restored at the King's insistence in 1781. Eleven years before, he had approved the plans by the Office of Works for the remodelling by Sir William Chambers of the Great Gatehouse on the West Front, because of its highly unstable condition. One of the glories of Wolsey's palace, the towering brick edifice was reduced in height by two storeys, and Chambers made the central part of the tower (previously flanked by much taller turrets with domes) into the highest element in the new design.

139. (previous pages) John Spyers, North view of the Vases by the Royal Palace at Hampton Court *(detail), c. 1780; see fig. 142.*

140. (opposite, top) John Spyers, A View of the Green House Garden, taken at the Green House Gate, *c. 1780. This is the Privy Garden looking south, after Lancelot 'Capability' Brown allowed the trees to grow naturally out of their clipped shape.*

141. (opposite, bottom) John Spyers, The Middle of the Wilderness Garden at Hampton Court, *c. 1780. The Maze, which formed part of the Wilderness, has been a source of delight and consternation to visitors from Daniel Defoe to Jerome K. Jerome and Paddington Bear.*

The 'Grace-and-Favour' Palace after 1760

142. *John Spyers,* North view of the Vases by the Royal Palace at Hampton Court, c. 1780. *Access to the gardens had been restricted while the royal family still used the palace, but after 1760 the Wilderness and Great Fountain Garden were opened up to 'respectable people'.*

143. *Lancelot 'Capability' Brown by Sir Nathaniel Dance-Holland, c. 1769. As royal gardener, he was entitled to live in Wilderness House, north of the palace.*

Meanwhile, Lancelot 'Capability' Brown (fig. 143), who had been made Head Gardener at Hampton Court in 1764, had royal blessing for his policies. He retained the layout and structure of the palace gardens instead of sweeping away the older formality as he did in other places, but allowed a more naturalistic form to emerge. He achieved that simply by no longer cutting the topiary. The result may have seemed more natural to him, but to many visitors it just looked unkempt (fig. 140). Brown's most famous and most lasting contribution

144. *John Spyers,* The East View of the Second Inferior Court, c. 1780. *Master Carpenter's Court looking east. The windows and chimneys show the progressive 'Georgianization' of the building, although service areas like this remained relatively untouched.*

was to plant the Great Vine in 1768, which has long been one of the biggest attractions at the palace (fig. 145). A cutting from an already old Black Hamburg grape at Valentines Mansion, Essex, the Great Vine was given its own vinehouse in the south-west corner of the Pond Gardens. (This has since been extended or rebuilt on various occasions as the vine has grown, the last time being in 1964.) Even thirty years after it was planted, its branches had already filled the allotted space, 22 metres long by 5.5 metres wide (72 × 18 ft), and yielded 1800 bunches of grapes.

Palace residents

George III and his wife, Charlotte of Mecklenburg-Strelitz, came to Hampton Court from time to time, visiting former courtiers who resided there, and the King held occasional audiences in the State Apartments throughout his reign. There were further rounds of royal visits after 1795, to the King's cousin William V, Prince of Orange. Forced to flee from The Netherlands ahead of the French Revolutionary armies, the Prince was granted the use of apartments on the East Front of the palace, together with the Queen's Guard and Presence Chambers on the floor above. A figure of fun for his rotund shape and his amorous activities (fig. 146), the Prince of Orange returned to his homeland after the Peace of Amiens in 1802.

The Prince was by no means the only person to live at Hampton Court, although he had a more privileged and better appointed home

145. Harvesting the Great Vine in August 1960. The vine produces an annual crop of black eating grapes of around 300 kilograms (660 lb), which are sold to visitors in the palace shops in late summer.

146. William V of Orange's busy pursuit of the opposite sex was caricatured in an etching by James Gilray in 1796. Lord Holland wrote, 'When the Prince of Orange resided at Hampton Court, his amours with the servant-maids were supposed to be very numerous.'

than others. In the 1740s, a select but often poor group of courtiers had been given the privilege of residing there in the summer months. From this stemmed the practice of residence 'by the grace and favour' of the sovereign, and the palace was progressively divided into a series of apartments for those deserving of assistance. Beginning formally in 1767 and organized under official warrants from 1773, the practice lasted almost to the close of the twentieth century.

'Grace and favour'

Hannah More, the moralizing author, noted on a visit in 1770 that 'the private apartments are almost full, they are occupied by people of fashion, mostly of quality'. William Brummell, the father of 'Beau' Brummell (the king of fashionable Bath), was among them and he occupied an apartment from 1772. Dr Samuel Johnson was famously refused an apartment four years later, on the grounds that the waiting list was now full. Practice shifted by degrees, and by the 1840s the palace was almost exclusively the residence of widows whose husbands had served with distinction in military or imperial service but who had often fallen on harder times.

Over time, the palace was divided into more than fifty grace-and-favour apartments; some were dozens of rooms in extent, others much smaller. A parliamentary review in 1842 recorded between sixty and seventy households in the palace and its attendant buildings, with 150 to 200 servants between them. Only a few years before, William IV had called his near-forgotten palace 'the quality poor-house'. Charles Dickens characterized the residents as 'civilized gypsies' in his novel *Little Dorrit* (1857):

> *There was a temporary air about their establishments, as if they were going away the moment they could get anything better; there was also a dissatisfied air about themselves, as if they took it very ill that they had not already got something much better.*

Despite their size and seeming grandeur, these apartments often lacked basic amenities such as water closets, sewage, kitchens located within easy reach of dining rooms, and, later, gas and electricity. Slowly the palace was brought closer to contemporary living standards, although even as late as the mid-twentieth century a 105-year-old resident was refused permission to install a bathroom. Not only were there complaints and disputes about amenities between residents

147. Intrepid Edwardian ladies climbing on to the roof of the Great Hall in September 1905. This photograph is taken from an album belonging to Madeline Keyes, granddaughter of Lady Keyes, who was resident in Apartment 30 from 1902 to 1916.

The Story of Hampton Court Palace

and the relevant authorities – the Lord Chamberlain and the Board of Works being the main ones – but also friction over such matters as rank and precedence. There was continuing rancour over the seating arrangements within the Chapel Royal, the keeping of pets, the use of the gardens, and relations with the growing bands of paying visitors.

Of these, the greatest difficulties were in the Chapel. Worshippers sat strictly by rank and social standing, policed by the resident housekeeper. There was sometimes unseemly behaviour when elderly ladies tried to pull rank over their neighbours or over visitors to the Chapel. The problem of seating had become so urgent that in 1866 the architect Anthony Salvin reordered the pews and added a block of box pews in the centre. Even with these enhancements the disputes continued, until the Lord Chamberlain decreed that no longer were residents to sit by rank.

Pets were another cause of serious friction between residents and the housekeeper. In 1880 the residents petitioned the Lord Chamberlain to change the rule that dogs were not allowed to be kept in the palace. As a concession, he permitted the keeping of 'lap

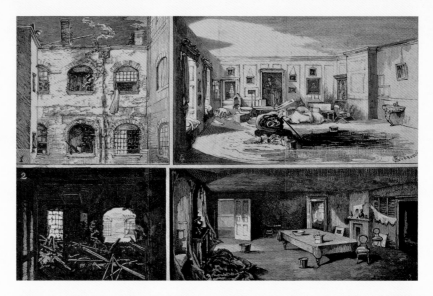

148. (top right) The fire of 1882 at Hampton Court, graphically reported in the Illustrated London News. *The fire broke out in a grace-and-favour apartment above the Queen's Gallery; the cause was found to be 'the overflowing of the burning spirit in a small spirit lamp'. An ever-present danger, fire also offered the opportunity to rebuild in appropriately Tudor style.*

149. (right) The 'painted room' in the Banqueting House during the occupation of Mrs Mary Campbell, 1936. After her death in 1945, the Banqueting House was opened to the public. Earlier residents ensured that the paintings, with naked figures of the gods, were covered with bookcases or fabric to spare their blushes.

dogs'. This definition, however, was widely exploited as ladies gave promises that their lap dog – perhaps a German shepherd or golden retriever – was extremely well behaved.

Occasional rogues as well as the families of daring explorers and devoted servants of Empire occupied the apartments. Lord and Lady Henry Gordon, who lived in an apartment overlooking Fountain Court from 1850, were constantly being reprimanded for misconduct. The family's fortunes worsened; in 1865 Lord Gordon was declared bankrupt and bailiffs seized almost all of the family's furniture. Lord Gordon disappeared, but Lady Gordon and her family took refuge in another apartment for two years before she died.

In 1864 Miss Baly, a new grace-and-favour resident of the Banqueting House in the south gardens, was horrified to find that the rooms were decorated with naked figures (fig. 149). She wrote

to the Lord Chamberlain, 'I find very objectionable the large undressed figures in the frescoes on each side of the fireplace and venture to suggest that they should be either draped or clouded in such a manner as render them appropriate decorations for a drawing room.' Her wish was granted, and only in 1945 were the Baroque wall paintings uncovered once more.

Minor royal residents continued to come to live in the palace. Elizabeth Emily FitzClarence, one of ten illegitimate children fathered by William IV before he came to the throne, lived on the ground floor of the East Front of the palace in the 1830s. In the 1880s another resident was Princess Frederica of Hanover, a descendant of George II. Following the early death of her daughter, she founded a home nearby for poor and delicate married women recovering from childbirth, for which she held fundraising evenings of entertainment in the Great Hall (fig. 150). She also made one of the last major additions to the built fabric of the main palace: an extension of her apartments, situated in the south-west corner. (The Clore Learning Centre at the

Barrack Block, designed by Feilden Clegg Bradley and opened in 2006, is the only modern addition since.)

More exotic were several of the children of Maharajah Duleep Singh, the Sikh leader who had been brought to Britain as a boy in 1849 after the Second Anglo-Sikh War. Princess Sophia Duleep Singh and other members of her immediate family (fig. 151) lived in Faraday House, opposite Hampton Court Green. A prominent suffragette, she often went on protest demonstrations in the years before the First World War. Others involved in the struggle for the vote threatened to bring their fight to the palace. In February 1913 Hampton Court was closed to the public for seven months 'owing to the fear of damage by women suffragists', and extra policemen were posted on guard. In the 1930s the Princess wrote to the Lord Chamberlain's office requesting certain improvements, including the installation of electricity. This was ironic, as a previous grace-and-favour tenant of the same house was Michael Faraday, whose research had laid the foundations of the exploitation of electricity.

In 1936 a Russian royal refugee came to live at the palace with her family. The Grand Duchess Xenia Alexandrovna was the sister of the assassinated Tsar Nicholas II and widow of Alexander Mikhailovich, Grand Duke of Russia. She remained in Wilderness House, close to the Maze, until her death in 1960. Among the best-known twentieth-century residents until the 1970s was Olave, Lady Baden-Powell, widow of the

151. Princesses Bamba and Catherine Duleep Singh, eldest daughters of the Maharaja Duleep Singh, who were granted tenancy of Faraday House with their sister Sophia in 1896. Later, both became notable members of the suffragette movement in the years of women's struggle for the vote before the First World War.

152. Field Marshal Viscount Wolseley, victor of the Zulu Wars, photographed in Apartment 39, c. 1910. He resided in the palace from 1899 to his death in 1913; his widow transformed the apartment into a memorial to him.

founder of the Boy Scouts and herself the head of the Girl Guides movement. No stranger to the palace, since her friend Lady Manning already occupied a forty-room apartment on the West Front, Lady Baden-Powell was given an apartment in 1942, as her own home had been commandeered 'for the duration' of the Second World War. Aged fifty-three, she was the youngest grace-and-favour resident. Past and present Girl Guides from all over the world came to see her there. Her sixteen-room apartment (fig. 154) extended from the Great Hall northwards and incorporated significant parts of Henry VIII's Great Kitchen. One huge fireplace had even been converted into a bathroom.

153. (above) A rare view of the interior of a grace-and-favour apartment, 1937. Mrs Barbara Cecil Brooke lived there at the time; following her death in 1979 the apartment was home to the Textile Conservation Centre until 1999.

154. A reproduction Tudor room in Lady Baden-Powell's apartment annexe, 1976. The three-storey annexe filled the western half of the Great Kitchen and was dismantled in 1978.

Only two palace residents remain, and the practice of granting new tenancies ceased in 1969. The legacy continues to this day, not least in the deliveries baskets, name-plates, bells and door numbers that survive in almost every corner, as well as the staff that live in the palace, including the Vine Keeper, Head Gardener and Chaplain.

Rediscovering the Antique

The long saga of grace-and-favour residence was played out against the story of works and architectural discovery at Hampton Court Palace.

Anthony Salvin, who worked in the Chapel Royal in the late 1860s to solve the residents' seating problems, was but one architect of distinction who was employed there. A roll call of English architects and designers left their mark, following in the footsteps of Chambers. When Chambers had essayed the gothic style, on the Great Gatehouse, it had been half-hearted. James Wyatt and his Clerk of Works Thomas Hardwick embraced the ancient style with enthusiasm and began the lengthy process of turning the clock back at the palace, uncovering and restoring earlier fabric. On the King's orders in 1800, Wyatt removed the theatre from the Great Hall,

revealing the Tudor interior not seen for a century (fig. 155). Wyatt began the process of making the Great Hall even more Tudor than it had ever been, opening a new doorway from the dais into the Great Watching Chamber in an exemplary copy of the arched doorway in the adjacent Horn Room.

Hampton Court was on the cusp of change. One of the dominant themes there in the nineteenth century was the rediscovery of Tudor architecture, putting back the Tudor elements that had been lost, and sometimes embellishing them further. The architecture of the sixteenth century had come to seem debased, having neither the full glory of the medieval Gothic nor the purity of the revived classical style. In the opening decades of the nineteenth century this attitude changed, and Hampton Court was in part both cause and beneficiary. A.C. Pugin's *Specimens of Gothic Architecture* (1821–23) contained the first detailed measured drawings of the Great Hall and its roof, while Joseph Nash began the romanticizing of the Tudor court in its proper setting in the illustrations to his *Mansions of England in the Olden Time* (1839–49; fig. 6).

William IV (1830–37) succeeded his brother George IV (1820–30), whose main effect on the palace had been to strip the gardens of much of their statuary. From that date the antiquarian approach to Hampton

155. Gothic Hall (the Great Hall) by W.J. Bennet after Charles Wild, from W.H. Pyne's History of the Royal Residences *(1819). The Tudor hall, stripped of its fittings as a theatre, is revealed once more.*

156. The Great Hall looking east in c. 1890, incorporating the changes made by Edward Jesse to make the room more romantically Tudor, although there is no evidence that armour had ever been previously hung in the hall. This arrangement survived until 1925.

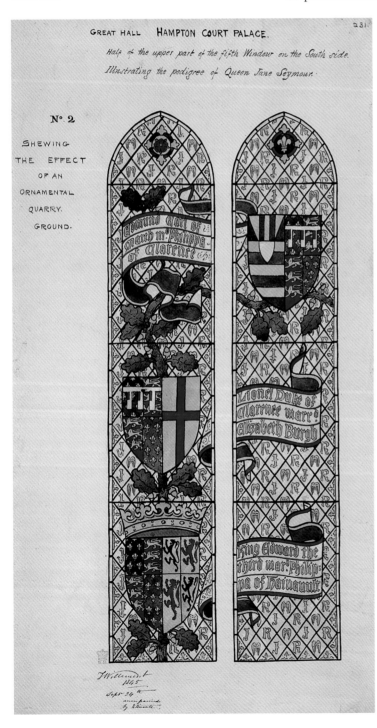

157. Thomas Willement's design for a stained-glass window in the Great Hall, 1845, here illustrating the pedigree of Queen Jane Seymour. The stained glass was but one element in the redecoration of the Tudor hall.

Court took firm hold. Edward Jesse, appointed Itinerant Deputy Surveyor in the Office of Woods, Forests and Land Revenues in 1834, had a particular and lasting effect on the palace over the succeeding twenty years. With a deep romanticism and affection for gothic styles and picturesque irregularity – and with an equally deep distaste for Wren and the Baroque – Jesse supervised a series of restorations and re-presentations. The most notable was that of the Great Hall itself (fig. 156). Left clear and relatively bare by Wyatt, it was transformed between 1840 and 1846 into a state that Jesse believed Cardinal Wolsey and Henry VIII would have recognized instantly. The great series of Abraham tapestries, one of the glories to have survived from Henry VIII's reign, was returned from the King's State Apartments. The hammerbeam ceiling was repainted and the windows of the Great Hall and the Great Watching Chamber were filled with stained glass designed by Thomas Willement (fig. 157). Heraldic badges and figures in the glass evoked the genealogy of Henry VIII, his wives and family, and his Chancellor, Thomas Wolsey. Artful arrangements of arms and armour were placed around the walls on specially constructed corbels, and deer antlers (all from the parks) were added for further effect. When Jesse had finished, it was 'probably the finest and most brilliantly embellished building in Europe', in the words of the correspondent of the *Gentleman's Magazine*.

Jesse continued in the same manner wherever he had opportunity. The ceiling of the Chapel Royal (painted white in the reign of Queen Anne) was repainted in its original rich blue colouring and gilded with gold stars. With Edward Blore as supervising architect, considerable changes were made to the palace exterior in the course of the 1840s. First the West Front and then its projecting wings were returned to their original appearance by the replacement of Georgian sash windows with Tudor-style casements (fig. 158). The restoration was universally acclaimed; similar programmes of work followed in Clock Court, Base Court and

Master Carpenter's Court. Attention then turned to the decayed and miscellaneous collection of chimneys. These too were replaced, often in more fantastic shapes than had ever been there originally but based on surviving examples found at other sixteenth-century English houses. Only the brighter brick distinguished much of this Victorian work from the original; the mortar was artificially blackened with ash and soot, to match the now discoloured Tudor mortar (leaving problems that are still being resolved in the present day).

The impetus behind all this work was not simply the result of a successful antiquarian campaign, and it was certainly not done to please the growing grace-and-favour resident population. As the public were admitted from 1838, the privileged few were replaced by the many. They were all keen to see not only the gardens, the magnificent art collection and the State Apartments, but also the considerably more romantic Tudor parts of the palace. Visitor demand and antiquarian romance coincided. In many ways, they still do.

158. Woolnoth after J.P. Neale, The Entrance to Hampton Court Palace, *1814. Many of the Georgian sash windows were soon to be comprehensively replaced in the great campaign of 'Tudorization' that was intended to return the palace to its supposed appearance in its heyday.*

The 'Grace-and-Favour' Palace after 1760

The Maze, Hampton Court Palace.

The Visitor's Hampton Court from 1838

In 1838, in an early act of generosity towards her public, the young Queen Victoria (1837–1901), niece of George IV and William IV, ordered that Hampton Court Palace 'should be thrown open to all her subjects without restriction'. The death of the Lady Housekeeper, Lady Emily Montague, provided the opportunity for public access; the position was abolished along with the shilling (5 pence) entrance fee. In the eighteenth century and even earlier, visitors of social standing had been admitted by paying a fee to the resident housekeeper, who conducted them around at some speed, pointing out Old Master paintings and artefacts such as Cardinal Wolsey's supposed (and oversized) shoe. This new direction smacked of democracy.

The spirit of revolution was still abroad in Europe. Some commentators had visions 'of an insulting rabble, such as that which invaded the Tuileries in the time of Louis XVI, marching through the State Apartments, tearing down the tapestries, wrecking the furniture, and carrying off pictures'. The grace-and-favour residents were also unhappy at the prospect of being overrun by hordes of visitors. The apprehensions about revolutionaries were ill-founded, although the resident population did come to feel under siege as hundreds of thousands were visiting each year by the middle of the nineteenth century. In nearly 200 years the flow of visitors has never ceased (fig. 160).

The palace was a 'well-loved resort of cockneydom', in the words of the novelist Anthony Trollope. Sunday was the favoured day, when house and grounds were frequently overrun. The Victorian travel writer William Howitt thought that Hampton Court was 'one of the bravest pleasures that a party of happy friends can promise themselves'. The Hampton Court area and the river became the focus of pleasure seekers, with sailing races and more leisurely boating on the river, the expansion of the nearby villages, and the open parks. The most celebrated nineteenth-century fictional visitors to the palace were Jerome K. Jerome's *Three Men in a Boat* of 1889. In the novel, Harris recounted to his two companions – not forgetting the dog, Montmorency – the story of a previous visit when he and a group of others became hopelessly lost in the Maze (which was then, as now, one of the principal attractions in the palace grounds; fig. 163).

159. (previous pages) Edwardian visitors in the Maze; see fig. 163.

160. (below) The throng of visitors in Base Court, c. 1936, including some who appear to have taken a dip in the Thames before arriving.

161. (opposite) Detail of a London Transport poster by Clive Gardiner, 1927, one of many from the 1900s to the 1950s advertising the delights of Hampton Court. The system of buses, trams and trolley-buses brought the great majority of visitors in the interwar years.

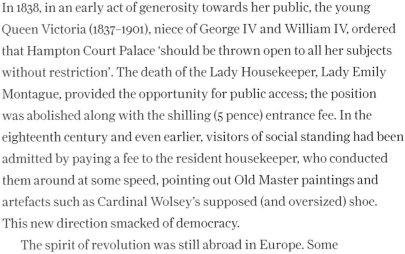

The Visitor's Hampton Court from 1838

The Maze, Hampton Court Palace.

162. *Indian visitors in Home Park in 1902, when a large contingent from the Indian Army was encamped there. A military presence in and around the palace lasted until the Second World War.*

163. *Edwardian visitors in the Maze, one of the great draws for visitors to the palace gardens since the eighteenth century and a scene of frequent frustration.*

164. *Private cars parked on the West Front in 1928. The pressure for parking space is nothing new. To remove this eyesore and to protect the building, a new car park was opened behind the Barrack Block in 1930.*

This humorous episode was balanced by another passage in Jerome's description of the visit, celebrating the antique beauty of the place:

What a dear old wall that is that runs along by the river there! ... There are fifty shades and tints and hues in every ten yards of that old wall. ... I've often thought I should like to live at Hampton Court. It looks so peaceful and so quiet, and it is such a dear old place to ramble round in the early morning before many people are about.

Guidebooks increased in number when the palace was opened fully to the public. The tireless Edward Jesse not only supervised works in the palace but also wrote hugely successful guides. *Gleanings in Natural History* appeared in 1835, *A Summer's Day at Hampton Court* four years later. The first was concerned more with natural phenomena, and particular pride of place was given to the giant Cardinal spiders that are peculiar to the palace and its park. The second gave detailed itineraries to and from central London, as well as descriptions of the principal attractions at and around the palace.

Increased leisure time and improved transport spurred the growth in nineteenth-century tourism. An astonishing total of 10 million visitors had come to the palace by 1881, sped there by new forms of transport as well as by curiosity. In the 1830s the horse-drawn omnibus departed from central London every twenty minutes. In 1849 the London and

South-Western Railway opened its branch line to Hampton Court, terminating at Sir William Tite's neo-Jacobean station building. In the early twentieth century, visitors could come from Hammersmith by tram, and later by trolley-bus (fig. 161). There were always river trips available, and the rise of the motor omnibus and subsequently the private car made Hampton Court increasingly accessible to all (fig. 164).

The peak times for visitors coincided particularly with the displays of flowers in the gardens and parks: horse chestnuts, daffodils, tulips or rhododendrons. An increasing range of facilities was available to them: lavatories and a small shop had been added within the palace by the 1870s, while there were nine hotels and two restaurants at the gates. As transport made it ever easier to come to Hampton Court, the Bank Holiday Act of 1871 gave new occasions for visiting. It was also held responsible for a widely deplored increase in 'rowdy and bawdy behaviour'. In the 1880s palace residents were complaining that indecent (nude) bathing in the river added to their burden from visitors. By the close of the century, many were complaining about the 'loose women' who gathered around the soldiers quartered in the Barrack Block beside Trophy Gate.

Interior displays

Inside the palace, the considerable wear and tear on the buildings from the tide of visitors meant that various changes needed to be made from the 1850s. There was comprehensive reflooring in the most heavily trafficked areas with tiles and other more durable but inauthentic materials. Metal barriers and even grilles were erected to protect vulnerable pictures and furnishings (fig. 165). There were always many visitors who came to enjoy the treasured paintings hanging on the walls. Gradually, the palace had become a crowded art gallery as much as, if not more than, a historic house.

When Queen Victoria opened the palace to all, Ernest Law wrote, 'the thirty-two rooms of the state apartments exhibited a strange heterogeneous conglomeration of a thousand pictures of every value, of every period and of every school, hung up anyhow and everywhere, just as they came'. A considerable part of the work undertaken during the course of the nineteenth century, and since, has been to return the palace and its contents to order.

165. (above) Protective grilles around furniture in the Queen's Audience Chamber, photographed in the 1920s or earlier. Although security measures were and remain a necessity, in many parts of the palace the late Victorian arrangements seem excessive to modern eyes.

166. One of the Royal Engineers' crates for transporting the Raphael cartoons to the Victoria and Albert Museum in 1865. When it became known that the cartoons were to be moved to South Kensington, the palace inhabitants petitioned the House of Lords that the cartoons stay, but to no avail.

The Visitor's Hampton Court from 1838

Among the most glorious of the palace's treasures were the Raphael cartoons for the tapestry series of the *Acts of the Apostles*. Taken away in 1763, but returned to Hampton Court in 1804, they were one of the high points of the public tour. The constant moving of the fragile cartoons was seen as a threat to their survival and in 1865 they were removed in massive crates to the Victoria and Albert Museum in South Kensington, where they still hang (fig. 166). This was part of a controversial deal struck with the museum's founder, Henry Cole. Most of the other objects he took were returned in due course, but Cole's prize acquisition of the cartoon series remains in the museum.

Richard Redgrave, Surveyor of the Royal Pictures and a close friend of Cole, took the opportunity to undertake a major reorganization of the paintings at Hampton Court in the course of the 1860s. The Mantegna *Triumphs of Caesar* paintings were moved to the Communication Gallery, where special floor traps were installed for their swift removal in the event of fire. Major discoveries were made on the way: the Alexander tapestries in the Queen's Gallery were uncovered from beneath papered linen. Alongside these changes there was a considerable reordering, making the interior more of a museum than a palace. Tapestries were removed from the walls of the State Apartments to other rooms. The collections were grouped and regrouped on didactic rather than historical principles. The Queen's Private Dining Room became a bed museum, containing Queen Caroline's state bed, George II's travelling bed and William III's state bed all in a row (fig. 167).

In his book of 1897 on Hampton Court, William Holden Hutton described the palace's

167. (above) The 'bed museum' in the Queen's Private Dining Room: left to right, Queen Caroline's state bed, George II's travelling bed and William III's state bed. One feature of the twentieth-century trend for authentic and appropriate room presentation was to return furnishings to their proper setting. These beds were all moved in the major re-presentation of the 1930s.

168. A typical Victorian postcard of 'The Hampton Court Palace Ghost' in the Great Hall. The card describes how the ghost of Catherine Howard stops suddenly, 'and wringing her hands shrieks despairingly, then returns and disappears at the entrance to the haunted chamber'.

The Hampton Court Palace Ghost.
The Ghost of Catherine Howard, wife of Henry VIII, said to be seen at night rushing through the Great Hall. She stops suddenly, and wringing her hands shrieks despairingly, then returns and disappears at the entrance to the haunted chamber.

The Story of Hampton Court Palace

dual appeal. It was a 'holiday-ground for thousands of Londoners', but it was also a 'world invisible or half known' filled with history where 'imagination and tradition vie in bringing forth tales of strange noises and mysterious presences'. The bestselling picture postcards of Hampton Court in the decades around 1900 were of ghostly spectres in various of the historic spaces (fig. 168). It was little matter that these were obvious fakes; the palace famously had ghosts and these images were as close as most visitors would get to any evidence for them. The legend of the ghost of Queen Catherine Howard, eternally rushing along the Haunted Gallery to plead for her life, was the best-known example, but ectoplasmic encounters were expected around every corner.

Interest in the spectral presences at the palace continues almost unabated. When a possible ghost was captured on a closed-circuit television camera in 2003, the news went round the world; night-time winter ghost tours sell out every time they are advertised.

Restoration

The closing decades of the nineteenth century witnessed not only popular interest in palace ghosts but also renewed attention to the fabric and the grounds. The architect John Lessels worked on the restoration of both Hampton Court Palace and Windsor Castle. He gave the palace a reinforced Tudor appearance. The most publicly prominent of Lessels's works at Hampton Court were the extensive repairs to Anne Boleyn's Gateway and the Tudor Astronomical Clock, which was provided with a new mechanism in 1879, and the grassing over of Base Court. This was in the mistaken belief that it had originally been grass as it had been called Green Court, although that was because it was damp and often mossy. The restoration of the Great Gatehouse in 1882 (fig. 169) gave it its present-day appearance, with new shafts framing Sir William Chambers's central parapet and a new stone vault designed on the best antiquarian principles incorporating the arms of Queen Victoria and Cardinal Wolsey.

169. *Proposal for restoring the Great Gatehouse to its original height, 1882. This ambitious plan was eventually abandoned and a more modest scheme was undertaken, adding new shafts to the west façade and a stone vault beneath.*

THE KNOT GARDEN

COTTON LAVENDER.
THYME.
WINTER SAVORY.
LAVENDER.
BOX.
FLOWERS
PATHS.

The final touch was added when the original wooden doors were found and put back; they had been discovered as the floor of the palace carpenter's workshop.

Fire was a constant danger. The damage to rooms above the Queen's Gallery from a domestic fire in 1882 (fig. 148) paled into insignificance compared with the destruction of some seventy-five rooms on the North Front four years later. This provided an opportunity for Lessels to replace them with work that was even more clearly Tudor. Forty well-appointed new rooms were built specifically for grace-and-favour use, in contrast to other apartments that had been carved out of the older areas of the palace.

Lessels also continued the process of beautification of the palace interior, notably in the Horn Room and in extensive repairs to the ceiling of the Great Watching Chamber next door. He restored the so-called Wolsey Closet, with its enigmatic overlapping series of panel paintings, after it came into the public domain in 1886, when it ceased to be part of a grace-and-favour apartment. His work, whether designing a boiler-house built in a Tudor style or the refashioning of a coat of arms, was based on an archaeological sensitivity and architectural accuracy that had eluded many of his predecessors but set a new standard for his successors.

Gardens

By the end of the nineteenth century Hampton Court Palace was not only an object lesson in interior restoration but also was leading the fashion for colourful garden displays, notably carpet bedding. The East Front in particular was a riot of colour and crowded with bedding plants. Although the fashion waned and a greater variety of planting was introduced, the gardens remained a showcase for the style. Against this close-set planting was the vast, and influential, herbaceous border along the whole of the East Front gardens (fig. 172). Measuring 3 metres (10 ft) in width, and over 365 metres (1200 ft) in length, it was the

HAMPTON COURT PALACE
THE BLUE BORDER.

pride of the palace gardeners; it was – and remains – a draw for garden visitors (fig. 170).

The Hampton Court garden styles were much copied and admired; during the First World War, when the flower gardens were neglected, there was a general outcry. Once the wartime austerity was over, there were moves not only to restore the gardens to their colourful pre-war state but also to revive even earlier forms – or at least, design and plant 1920s interpretations of them. The Elizabethan Knot Garden and the Pond Gardens, both on the south side of the palace, were Ernest Law's proudest individual contributions to the gardening scene (fig. 171). The central Pond Garden was left looking, he believed, 'very much as it did when Henry VIII strolled therein with Anne Boleyn'. Although Law devoted considerable time and energy to understanding the history of the palace and gardens, his romantic sensibilities here as elsewhere often led him away from documentary reality. His description in 1891 of the Privy Garden is wrong on most counts, as much of what he described was either nineteenth-century or the result of allowing trees to grow unrestrained. Yet his planting schemes were an honest attempt to evoke the spirit of the place: 'These gardens retain, indeed, more perhaps of the form and spirit of former days than any others in England.'

As so often at Hampton Court Palace, the heart ruled the head. The romance and beauty of the place attracted both those who worked on the buildings and estate and those who visited. Archaeological accuracy and romance were interlinked. The twentieth century saw the process continuing, but with a shift in emphasis towards more 'correct' forms of presentation and display.

170. (above) Thomas Robert Macquoid, At Hampton Court, *c. 1860. Visitors flocked to enjoy the East Front gardens, and by the mid-nineteenth century up to 180,000 people a year were visiting the palace.*

171. (opposite, top) Design for the Knot Garden by Ernest Law, 1924. Law had already designed a similar garden for Shakespeare's house at Stratford-upon-Avon. For more than thirty years his influence extended to every aspect of the palace, its history and decoration.

172. (opposite, bottom) The Blue Border in the East Front gardens, depicted in 1913. By the late nineteenth century the palace gardens had become famous for their brightly coloured flower borders and carpet bedding.

Conservation in the Twentieth Century and Beyond

Each generation has recast Hampton Court in its own image. In the course of the twentieth century, tastes and sensibilities changed, reflected at each stage in the development of the buildings and the gardens. The emphasis now has moved gradually away from restoration of what was once there (or perhaps what it was felt *should* have been there) towards being informed and conserving as much as possible of what has survived.

The presiding genius over the palace for a generation was Ernest Law, self-appointed guardian of Hampton Court and its history from the close of the nineteenth century until his death in 1930. A former solicitor and himself a grace-and-favour resident in the Pavilion in Home Park, he invested every ounce of his energy in the palace he loved. His touch was everywhere. He planned and implemented new forms of presentation and visitor amenities. He supervised archaeology and the reconstruction of parts of the building and the gardens. He wrote palace guidebooks (an activity in which he enjoyed a monopoly). In 1885–89 he had published his magisterial three-volume history of Hampton Court, which remained until 2003 the most significant study of the palace.

One of the most apparent of Law's legacies is the moat and the reclaimed bridge that provides the principal entrance to the palace at the Great Gatehouse. The moat had been filled in as part of the works undertaken for William and Mary, in order to make a grand circular turning sweep for carriages. In 1909 it was decided to investigate and if possible reinstate both moat and bridge (fig. 174). Most of the bridge had in fact survived except its parapets, and these were restored complete with ten newly carved Tudor heraldic beasts to the plan described in the original building accounts (fig. 175). (These carvings weathered badly, and the present beasts date from 1950.) The parapets include discarded Tudor bricks found in the moat. The gatehouse itself was refaced again, in a more mellow brick than before. The century was opening at Hampton Court as it would continue, with a new emphasis on archaeology and the reuse of historic material.

Law was also instrumental in opening up more areas inside the palace for visitors (fig. 176), especially in the Tudor parts, passing out of the Great Hall via the Horn Room through the Great Watching Chamber and along the Haunted Gallery to the Royal Pew. The antlers and horns displayed in the Horn Room were discovered in a heap at the foot of the serving stairs. Although they were resigned to the permanent public use of the Haunted Gallery, the grace-and-favour residents objected bitterly

173. *(previous pages) A blacksmith restores the Tijou screen in 1947; see fig. 183.*

174. *Excavation of the moat bridge underway in 1910. A trial hole in 1909 had confirmed the existence of features just below the surface.*

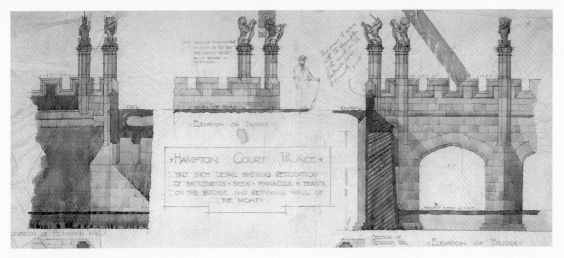

to the opening of the upper part of the Chapel Royal. Lady Rossmore shuddered at the prospect of the 'hundreds of dirty, smelly unwashed that will tramp through during the week', so fouling the space that 'we, none of us, could even try to sit any service out'.

The Great Hall was the object of the most thorough programme of works, after dry rot and beetle infestation were found in the roof in 1922. Decayed timbers were replaced and a steel truss system was inserted into the hammerbeam roof (fig. 177). The painted decoration

176. Early visitors to the Tudor Kitchens had little sense of the scale or uniqueness of their survival. Only when Lady Baden-Powell's grace-and-favour apartment in the western half was dismantled after she finally relinquished it in 1976 could the full extent of the ancient kitchen be appreciated.

177. *The palace's Clerk of Works with one of the bosses removed from the Great Hall roof during repairs in the 1920s. Bosses, carved heads and other decorative elements from the roof were stored and repaired in a workshop set up in the Upper Orangery in the King's Apartments while structural work was being carried out in the hall.*

178. *A workman examines the stonework on the turret of the Great Hall during the programme of repairs in 1936.*

on the timber was stripped away, as were many of the corbels, armour and other novelties that Edward Jesse had introduced in 1844. Almost as soon as the work on the Great Hall was completed, the roof of the Chapel Royal was found to be in a similarly decayed and dangerous state. Here, too, new structural supports were introduced to bear the weight of the Tudor timber ceiling.

Gradually, other parts of the palace were opened to public view: the Orangery in 1931; the Tennis Court in 1949; the Wolsey Rooms in 1951 (after an attempted opening in 1923 was halted following complaints that visitors' footsteps disturbed the resident below); the Cumberland Suite in 1963; and the Banqueting House in 1983. Styles of presentation of the historic spaces were also changing. No longer were the pictures on the walls the principal or even the sole objects of public and professional admiration. The palace's keepers and their advisers increasingly aimed to provide a more appropriate historic context for surviving grand and rare items of furniture, such as the state beds.

In addition to having a deep personal interest in Kensington Palace, Queen Mary, the wife of George V (1910–36), took a personal hand in Hampton Court. Considerable improvements were made in the course of the 1930s, culminating in a thorough re-presentation of the State Apartments on more historically appropriate lines. Sir Philip Sassoon gave the palace suitable furnishings, among them chairs of state to

179. *A palace admission ticket. The one-shilling (5 pence) entry charge was introduced in 1912 and survived until the post-1970 inflationary spiral. The palace has been open seven days a week since 1930.*

The Story of Hampton Court Palace

be placed in their proper setting beneath the throne canopies. He persuaded other philanthropists to provide improved amenities such as heating, ordered new wall hangings and rationalized the hitherto indiscriminate use of protective barriers. Kenneth Clark, Surveyor of the King's Pictures, supervised a thorough rehanging of the paintings. Elements of the basically chronological sequence that he devised still remain. In 1938, on the eve of war, Queen Mary attended a garden party to mark the centenary of the palace's opening to the public and the completion of this major re-presentation scheme.

The gardens remained the most popular attraction of the palace. The glorious if labour-intensive borders and beds with their seasonal displays drew crowds of admirers. The largest new addition to the public areas came with the opening of the Tiltyard Gardens in 1925 (fig. 181). Originally the site of the Tudor jousting arena, from which a single brick viewing tower has survived, the 3.2 hectares (8 acres) had become a royal kitchen and fruit garden in the reigns of William III and Anne. In the late nineteenth century, after the palace gardens had ceased to provide food for the royal table, the Tiltyard was leased to a successful nursery, which provided the vast numbers of plants required annually for the famous bedding displays. Eventually the lease was terminated, in order to make the Tiltyard into a new visitor amenity with tennis courts, tea-rooms and new garden displays. The tea-rooms and cafeteria were the most successful element in the scheme, and their successor (built in 1964 and refurbished in 1995) still welcomes visitors. The car park on the former parade ground behind the Barrack Block opened in 1930, removing the serried ranks of cars and charabancs previously parked at the West Front (fig. 164).

In the wider estate, Home Park had been opened to the public in 1893, when it finally ceased to be a royal stud. It soon acquired both a public golf course and a model yacht pond, each with a clubhouse. Bushy Park, a focus of Chestnut Sunday gatherings and penny-farthing bicycle races, had been open for well over half a century.

Both parks were extensively used for growing crops in each of the world wars, as were the palace gardens. In the Second World War, anti-glider trenches were dug in Home Park to deter enemy landings, and the palace was the target of a number of (largely unsuccessful) bombing raids. The worst was when up to 300 incendiary bombs fell on the

180. (above) The palace electricity master board in 1954. Gradually every modern convenience has been added to the ancient building, from sewers, gas and electricity to computer cabling.

181. Lawn tennis in the Tiltyard Gardens in the 1920s, drawn by A. Forestier. A new recreation centre was created in the Tiltyard and opened to the public in 1925. It included tennis courts, a putting green and a new tea house in the Tiltyard Tower.

East Front on the night of 26 September 1940, although most were swiftly extinguished and damage was minimal. As a precaution, many important paintings were evacuated to safe locations, in particular the National Library of Wales at Aberystwyth, or were placed in secure stores, and a photographic record was made of important decorative elements. The US Eighth Army subsequently took over part of Bushy Park as its headquarters in 1942, and General Eisenhower planned the D-Day landings of 1944 there. The soldiers enjoyed being entertained in the palace – although some repaid the compliment by leaving their mark in the form of graffiti in sensitive areas such as the soft stonework in Fountain Court.

From living palace to ancient monument

Once the Second World War was over, the palace and grounds swiftly returned to their former role as an escape valve for many Londoners. Paintings came back from storage and more of the palace was opened up. Although facilities for visitors improved gradually over the postwar years, especially as leisure time expanded, there was demand for more. Change was in the air.

Ideas about historic houses were shifting, not least as England's stately homes were opening their doors and garden gates in order to make ends meet. In the visitor market for historic houses there was major competition. Meanwhile, the palace community itself was altering and shrinking. New tenants were not so easily found for grace-and-favour residences, while the total number of apartments was reduced both to save money and to be able to provide improved amenities for the remainder. Fewer of the residents kept servants. One symbol of change was that the infants' school in Tennis Court Lane closed its doors in 1953 (fig. 184).

Two highly significant and related decisions were made in 1969. First, the increasingly outmoded tradition of grace-and-favour residence would be allowed to draw to its natural close. With the rise of the welfare state and the demise of Empire it was seen as an anachronism, and no further apartments would be allocated or created.

182. (top) Restoration of the Verrio murals on the King's Staircase in 1968. The first restoration took place in the mid-eighteenth century, only twenty years after the paintings had been completed, and these delicate works have received attention at regular intervals since.

183. Restoring the Tijou screen in September 1947. A blacksmith's workshop was built around the individual screens, where all but the most sensitive work took place. The ironwork is exceptionally delicate, and there have been many repair schemes over its lifetime. The current scheme is partly complete.

Secondly, Hampton Court became an Ancient Monument and would no longer be considered a 'living' palace, so responsibility for its upkeep was to be transferred from the Royal Household to the Directorate of Ancient Monuments and Historic Buildings. In future, funding would be put towards the preservation of the 'unoccupied' palace within its setting and better presentation to the visiting public.

In-depth research, conservation measures for both the buildings and their contents, and a coherent approach to displaying the palace and gardens to the public all played their part in Hampton Court after 1969. Under a plan devised by Harold Yexley, senior architect in the Directorate of Ancient Monuments and Historic Buildings, some £2 million was to be spent between 1974 and 1980 on improving facilities, enhancing the historic spaces and completing the visitor routes. Various ways were found of using the increasing amounts of vacant space, whether by opening them to public view, taking in tenants with useful craft skills or as offices for palace staff. A more considered and historically inspired approach was taken to the display of the interiors, and especially the pictures. These included the enhanced presentation in 1975 of the prized and newly conserved Mantegna series of the *Triumphs of Caesar* in the Lower Orangery, new galleries for the reserve collection of paintings opened in 1980, and then in 1984 a dedicated Renaissance Picture Gallery.

In tandem, a more rigorously conservation-minded approach to the palace itself was adopted. One of the most visible results of the shift was – as usual for this building – in the brickwork. Brick repairs using mass-produced reproduction Tudor bricks had given many areas a wholly unfortunate new appearance. The repairs were in future to be carried out with handmade, traditional Bulmer bricks, bonded with lime mortar rather than Portland cement. A rolling programme of recording and making good the Tudor brickwork – often replacing inappropriate later work – continues to this day.

Fire and its aftermath

A watershed came in 1986. Before dawn on Easter Monday, 31 March, fire swept through the third floor and the roof on the South Front (fig. 185). It began in the apartment of Lady Gale,

184. Pupils of the palace infants' school in Tennis Court Lane, c. 1950. The school was established in 1876 and served the resident community until 1953.

185. Aerial view of the South Front showing the fire damage, 31 March 1986. Much of the roof, 60 metres (200 ft) long, had collapsed, sending timbers and molten lead crashing into the King's State Apartments below. Extensively fire-damaged and filled with waterlogged debris, the building was open to the elements and inherently unstable.

who lived above the King's State Apartments, and the lack of fire compartments in the roof void coupled with a failure of the alarm system allowed the blaze to race through the length of the building. Regrettably, Lady Gale perished in the fire, which may have been started by an unguarded candle flame in her bedroom.

The danger of fire had always been recognized – as early as 1716 wooden chimneypieces were being replaced by stone – and there had been major incidents before, notably in 1882, 1886 and again in 1952 in the Cumberland Suite (fig. 186). The palace had even had its own fire brigade (fig. 187), instituted in 1876 (but disbanded in 1955). None of these disasters matched the fire of 1986 in the seriousness of the damage. While firemen on twenty fire tenders were tackling the flames, a much-practised salvage operation swung into action to remove almost all of the valuable and portable works of art. The fire consumed only one table and one painting. News pictures of the scenes of devastation flashed round the world, showing leaping flames, and roof timbers and Grinling Gibbons limewood carvings in charred piles (fig. 188). By early afternoon, the fire had been extinguished and The Queen was touring the site to see the damage for herself.

The fire and its aftermath ushered in a further era of re-presentation and restoration at the palace, as well as a heightened awareness of the fragility and importance of its historic fabric. An archaeological approach was applied to the wreckage: for example, all fragments were meticulously examined and recorded, and many were rescued, repaired and reused despite the damage they had sustained. This approach proved to be a model for other historic properties, since the response to subsequent serious fires at Uppark, West Sussex, in 1989, and at Windsor Castle in 1992 drew on the Hampton Court experience. Detailed historical investigation, through archival

The Story of Hampton Court Palace

186. (far left) Firemen on the roof above the Cumberland Suite in 1952. One newspaper reported, 'Thirty titled women who live in the grace and favour apartments of the palace heard the crackling of burning wood just before 8 o'clock.'

187. The palace fire brigade on the West Front, 1954, made up from palace residents and local men to a full complement of nineteen.

research and archaeology, would henceforth precede and inform both repair and reconstruction.

The most visible and splendid fruit of that approach in the first half of the 1990s was the restoration and display of the King's Apartments themselves (figs. 189 and 190). This was accompanied by work on the Tudor Kitchens, the Cumberland Suite, the Queen's Private Apartments, and the 'Tudor route' in the rooms beyond the Great Hall. Mantegna's *Triumphs of Caesar* were redisplayed too, in a re-creation of the gallery at the Palace of San Sebastiano where they had originally hung. Finally came the restoration to its original form of the Privy Garden beneath the King's State Apartments.

These have been among the most influential changes in a major historic house in the modern age. In re-presenting the King's Apartments, there was opportunity to re-create the original form and decoration of the *enfilade* of rooms from the fairly public Guard Chamber to the very private bedchamber and study above, and then through the suites of more intimate rooms below. Furniture, paintings and tapestries were returned to the rooms for which they were originally intended. Historians in the 1980s were promoting the importance of spaces and their uses in the rituals of royal households as an expression of the politics that underpinned them. Here at Hampton Court was a unique opportunity to regain the ritual significance of the rooms, their disposition and decoration.

One of the most visible changes in the State Apartments was the rehanging of tapestries that had been dispersed long before, either elsewhere within the palace or to other royal houses, and replaced with wallpapers. The programme of cleaning and repair of these

188. The smouldering ruins of the Cartoon Gallery, 1 April 1986. Fortuitously, the Acts of the Apostles tapestries had been removed for cleaning prior to the fire. Reconstruction of the damaged interiors had to wait nearly three years to allow the building to dry out.

189. *The West Closet in the King's Private Apartments, photographed in 1982 in its last incarnation before the fully researched scheme of the early 1990s.*

190. *The West Closet in the King's Private Apartments, photographed in 1992. The re-presentation following the fire of 1986 returned the King's Apartments as close to their appearance in about 1700 as could be determined from archival and archaeological evidence.*

precious objects was the finest hour of the palace's Textile Conservation Studio, a body that could trace its origins back to William Morris's tapestry company three quarters of a century earlier (figs. 191 and 192). The fortuitous discovery and subsequent permanent loan of late seventeenth-century copies of the famed Raphael cartoons, which would hang in the restored Cartoon Gallery, released the *Acts of the Apostles* tapestries for display in the King's and Queen's Apartments.

These rooms were officially reopened by HM Queen Elizabeth II in July 1992. Just as influential were the Tudor Kitchens, opened to the public the previous year. In the 1970s they had been cleared of later insertions for grace-and-favour accommodation, revealing a kitchen block on a dramatic scale that has its origins in the very earliest Tudor house on the site. In more recent years a band of costumed kitchen

The Story of Hampton Court Palace

presenters and 'living archaeologists' has been contributing to both visitor enjoyment and knowledge about historic kitchen practices.

Once the work had been completed on the King's Apartments, attention turned to the Privy Garden outside. Allowed, then encouraged, over the years to become filled with overgrown trees and secluded walkways, this garden was also to be returned to its original glory. The scheme reunited the design of buildings and gardens for the first time in 250 years. The Victorian shrubs were felled, and important specimens were taken away for propagation or reuse. Archaeological excavations revealed that just below the surface still lay the bones of William III's great Baroque garden (fig. 193). Even the shapes of beds and borders could be discerned, while pictorial and documentary evidence provided the necessary detail.

191. Hampton Court's wet clean facility, housed in a converted greenhouse 24 metres (80 ft) in length to the north of the palace and used for washing tapestries. The late nineteenth-century policy of restoration of tapestries, even reweaving whole sections, has been superseded by a policy of painstaking cleaning and repair.

192. The tapestry restoration workshop was located in the Queen's Guard Chamber in the 1930s. Hampton Court Palace has been a world-leading centre for tapestry repair and conservation for more than a century.

193. (opposite) The restoration of the Privy Garden was a major, innovative exercise in garden archaeology. The garden was excavated in 1993–94 and discoveries included bed layouts, brick bases for statues, the central steps, tree pit positions and the entire original drainage system, which was repaired and returned to service.

194. William and Mary's palace had been conceived as the centrepiece of a great Baroque landscape. With the restoration of the Privy Garden in 1995, and for the first time in three centuries, it was possible to view the South Front as Wren intended and to see the river from the King's Apartments as William III had demanded.

Conservation in the Twentieth Century and Beyond

195. *The Jubilee Fountain at the far end of the Long Water, created to mark the Golden Jubilee of HM Queen Elizabeth II in 2002, is the largest multi-jet fountain in Britain.*

196. *The newly installed Kitchen Garden at Hampton Court opened in 2014, in the location of one of the kitchen gardens first established in the time of William III.*

197. *(below) Drama is now an integral part of the creative programme at Hampton Court. These young actors were part of the cast of Aphra Behn's saucy Restoration play* The Rover *in July 2012.*

Beginning in 1992, and completed three years later, the transformation was total and spectacular. Historic plant varieties were grown in Britain and The Netherlands. Some 33,000 box plants formed the edging to the beds cut into nearly 1 hectare (2.5 acres) of turf. Queen Mary's Bower was rebuilt in green oak on its high terrace to the west and replanted with hornbeam, replacements were carved for the original statuary (brought indoors for preservation), and a programme of restoration was begun on Tijou's screen on the river edge. In twenty years the gardens have matured into a scene that William III and Anne would have readily recognized (fig. 194).

The fame of the Hampton Court Palace gardens has continued to spread, while a more comprehensive strategy for care and renewal has been adopted since the late 1990s. The gardens are the home of the

National Collection of heliotropes, a quintessentially Victorian flower. The Cross Avenue and the Long Water Avenue in Home Park have both been replanted with lime trees of the appropriate species, descendants of the originals brought from The Netherlands in the later seventeenth century. The importance of the Baroque gardens is reflected in the reinstatement of Queen Mary II's prized collection of exotic plants, as well as a continuing programme to make replicas of the Delftware vases that she commissioned to display plants and flowers indoors. The Jubilee Fountain at the end of the Long Water was installed in 2002 (fig. 195), its five jets symbolizing the (then) five decades of The Queen's reign. Over the years the fountains in the gardens had been more troublesome than spectacular, suffering from lack of water pressure. Now that problem was overcome in fine fashion.

Historic Royal Palaces

Organizational change accompanied the new style of thinking and display. Nicholas Ridley, the chain-smoking Secretary of State for the Environment, had been trapped in the lift when visiting Hampton Court; when he was released he found that no single body could be found to be responsible for the palace. Following that incident, in 1989 the palace and the other 'unoccupied' royal palaces – the Tower of London, Kensington Palace State Apartments, Kew Palace with Queen Charlotte's Cottage, and the Banqueting House in Whitehall – came together under one body.

Historic Royal Palaces Agency was less constrained by the demands of Whitehall and the annual budget round. Hampton Court Palace was able to strike out more boldly and in new directions, among them the use of costumed guides to interpret the historic spaces for visitors (the first time the experiment had been tried at a major British site). Simon Thurley, the architectural historian appointed the Agency's first

198. *The palace hosted a series of events to mark the Diamond Jubilee of Queen Elizabeth II in 2012, including a 1950s-themed garden party that attracted over 16,000 people.*

199. *Bradley Wiggins leaves Hampton Court at the start of the men's cycling time trial of the London Olympics in 2012. He won the gold medal and was later pictured on the winner's golden throne in front of the palace.*

200. Cleaning the pendants on the ceiling of the Chapel Royal brings back life to one of the most fantastical legacies of the age of Henry VIII. Historic Royal Palaces has a team of conservators who use both traditional techniques and cutting-edge science in the guardianship of interiors and objects.

201. Excavations in Base Court in 2008 revealed the remains of the pre-Wolsey house on the site, predating any other finds made at the palace by nearly 200 years. The excavations were part of a project to re-present the Tudor courtyard in 2009 for the 500th anniversary of Henry VIII's accession to the throne.

Curator in 1989, led many of these projects and was a tireless advocate for the palace during his eight-year tenure. Greater distancing from direct government oversight has continued. After nine years, agency status ended and Historic Royal Palaces became an independent charity. It has a royal charter to pursue the twin goals of conservation and education – both broadly defined – in maintaining and presenting the major historic properties in its care (fig. 200).

The palace is the principal office location for Historic Royal Palaces. Some former grace-and-favour residences now house staff offices, and various long-standing tenants, notably the Royal School of Needlework, occupy other apartments. In the summer months Base Court is the venue for the Hampton Court Music Festival, and Home Park accommodates the annual Royal Horticultural Society's Hampton Court Palace Flower Show. Both maintain that tradition of popular entertainment alongside the historic attraction that has underpinned the visitor's experience since the nineteenth century.

Historic Royal Palaces continues to fulfil its charitable purposes in caring for these great buildings, through income from admissions, fundraising and retail profits. It has been in the forefront of exploring and developing new ways of showing historic places to the visiting public, whether that be audio guides, costumed interpreters, painstaking re-creations, drama or events such as the programme of works and displays with the celebrations of the 500th anniversary of Henry VIII's accession in 2009 (fig. 201) and the 300th anniversary of the Hanoverian succession in 2014 (fig. 202).

202. *The Queen's Apartments have been re-presented with dressed figures to help give a sense of their scale and the press of people when the court was in residence. Hampton Court Palace has frequently led the way in innovative forms of presentation of historic spaces.*

203. *Henry VIII's state crown was destroyed in 1649 after the Civil War; a meticulously researched copy was made by the Crown Jeweller in 2011 and has become a centrepiece of the Tudor displays at Hampton Court.*

Hampton Court Palace is a touchstone of English history. With the possible exception of Windsor Castle, nowhere else may visitors see the full complex of a surviving ancient royal palace. Certainly no other place may claim such an intimate relationship with Henry VIII (fig. 203), one of the most powerful and recognizable of English monarchs. Nowhere else in England does the full range of a Baroque royal palace survive. If William III and Mary II are less well known than their Tudor predecessors, their influence is internationally famous through the buildings and gardens at Hampton Court. The palace was built on a gigantic scale, both to reflect the status and glory of its owners and to accommodate a huge number of people when the royal court was in residence. Now it can accommodate half a million visitors or more each year.

Hampton Court Palace is history made visible.

Conservation in the Twentieth Century and Beyond

Further Reading

Index

Thomas Campbell, 'Cardinal Wolsey's Tapestry Collection', *The Antiquaries Journal*, vol. 76, March 1996, pp. 73–137

H.M. Colvin (ed.), *The History of the King's Works*, vol. IV (1982) and vol. V (1976), London (HMSO)

Brett Dolman, *Drama and Debate at the Court of James I*, Surrey (Historic Royal Palaces) 2004

Brett Dolman *et al.*, *Henry VIII: 500 Facts*, Surrey (Historic Royal Palaces) 2009

Jonathan Foyle, 'A Reconstruction of Thomas Wolsey's Great Hall at Hampton Court Palace', *Architectural History*, vol. 45, 2002, pp. 128–58; Daphne Ford and Michael Turner, 'The Kynges New Haull: A Response to Jonathan Foyle's "Reconstruction of Thomas Wolsey's Great Hall at Hampton Court Palace"', *Architectural History*, vol. 47, 2004, pp. 53–76

Ernest Law, *The History of Hampton Court Palace*, 3 vols, 2nd edn, London (George Bell & Sons) 1903

Philip Lindsay, *Hampton Court: A History*, London (Meridian) 1948

Todd Longstaffe-Gowan, *The Gardens and Parks at Hampton Court Palace*, London (Frances Lincoln) 2005

Sarah E. Parker, *Grace and Favour: The Hampton Court Palace Community, 1750–1950*, Surrey (Historic Royal Palaces) 2005

Simon Thurley, *Hampton Court: A Social and Architectural History*, New Haven, Conn., and London (Yale University Press) 2003

Simon Thurley (ed.), *The King's Privy Garden at Hampton Court Palace, 1689–1995*, London (Apollo Magazine/Historic Royal Palaces) 1995

The authors and publishers
would like to thank all those
members of the staff of Historic
Royal Palaces (HRP) and others
who have contributed in so
many ways to the preparation
of this book and its predecessor.
Particular thanks are due
to Anthony Geraghty, Tara
Hambling, Annie Heron,
Gordon Higgott, Edward Impey,
Todd Longstaffe-Gowan and
Simon Thurley; to colleagues
at the Royal Collections
Trust; to the Conservation
& Learning staff past and
present at HRP, especially
Tracy Borman, Brett Dolman,
Sebastian Edwards, Ruth
Gill, Alden Gregory, Susanne
Groom, Susan Holmes, Daniel
Jackson, Sarah Kilby, Sarah
Parker, Kent Rawlinson and Jo
Thwaites; and to many other
colleagues. Many thanks are
also due to Susan Mennell
for obtaining illustrations, to
Jonathan Foyle for drawing
the plans (front endpaper/
inside front cover), and to James
Brittain, Robin Forster (assisted
by Tim Whittaker and Ian
Forster) and Nick Guttridge
for photography. The authors'
special thanks go to Clare
Murphy, Publishing & Asset
Manager, for initiating and
managing the project.

Picture Credits

First published 2015 by Merrell Publishers,
London and New York

Merrell Publishers Limited
70 Cowcross Street
London EC1M 6EJ
merrellpublishers.com

in association with

Historic Royal Palaces
Hampton Court Palace
Surrey KT8 9AU
hrp.org.uk

Adapted with revisions from *Hampton Court
Palace: The Official Illustrated History*, first
published 2005

British Library Cataloguing in Publication Data.
A catalogue record for this book is available from
the British Library.

ISBN 978-1-8589-4631-3 (hardback)
ISBN 978-1-8589-4630-6 (paperback)

Produced by Merrell Publishers Limited
Designed by Nicola Bailey
Project-managed by Claire Chandler
Indexed by Hilary Bird

Printed and bound in China

Front jacket/cover:
West Front of the palace (see fig. 1)

Back jacket/cover (clockwise from top left):
East Front (see fig. 94); King's Staircase (see fig. 100);
Maze (see fig. 111); Chapel Royal (see fig. 117)

Frontispiece:
Philippe Mercier, The Music Party: Frederick,
Prince of Wales with his Three Eldest Sisters
(detail), c. 1733 (see fig. 133)

Pages 4–5, top to bottom:
Astronomical Clock (see fig. 58); Chapel Royal (see fig. 117);
Hendrick Danckerts, Hampton Court Palace *(detail),*
c. 1665–67 (see fig. 68); King's Staircase (see fig. 100);
Queen Caroline's Bathroom (see fig. 123); Maze (see fig. 111)